The Happy
Stay-at-Home Mom

How to Look &
Feel Amazing after
Having Your Baby

SARA GAVIRIA

Illustrations by Jamie Lee Reardin

The Happy Stay-at-Home Mom
Copyright © 2018 by Sara Gaviria
All rights reserved.

The information given in this book is intended as information and is not a substitute for medical advice. Please consult an appropriate physician for advice before implementing any of the suggestions of this book. While the author has made every effort to provide accurate internet addresses and product information at the time of publication, the author does not assume any responsibility for error or changes after publication.

Illustrations by Jamie Lee Reardin

Back Cover Photograph by Manny Perez Cover Design by 4Puntos

ISBN: 978-0-692-09061-9

Printed in United States of America

To my husband and my son

Table of Contents

Disclaimer vii

Introduction xi

Part 1: First Month

Welcome Home! 3

Common Conditions after Delivery 8

Breastfeeding 11

Me, My Baby, And My Waist Trainer 19

First Comes Love, Then Comes C-Section 22

Postpartum Depression 28

Part 2: Healthy Eating & Exercise

Month 1–2 37

Month 3 57

Month 6 65

Month 7–10 71

Month 11–12 75

Part 3: Beauty & Style

Skincare In 1, 2, 3 . . . 6 83

Body Care 99

Lose Stress, Not Your Hair 104

Homemade Treatments 109

Makeup vs Natural and Everything in Between 116

When In Doubt, Wear Sunglasses 123

Beauty Sleep is Not a Myth 133

Part 4: Hello World, What Did I Miss?

Find Your Tribe 143

Your Time Is Precious—Organize It. 150

Shape Your Husband Like a Rough Diamond 156

Keep Up With The World 160

If You Don't Love It, Leave It! 165

Meditation And Mindfulness. 169

The Yoga Way 174

Join a Group 180

Reconnect with Nature and Take Your City by Storm . . 181

Make Memories. 183

Make Time To Play 185

Find Your Passion 189

Final Words. 195

The 12-Month Checklist 199

Happiness Challenge 203

Acknowledgments 205

Book Recommendations 209

Bibliography 215

About the Author 223

Disclaimer

I moved to London when I was 22 years old. In one of my email conversations with my mom, I told her that I was reading a book about Buddhism, and within five minutes, my dad called to remind me I was Catholic, Apostolic, and Roman. I said: "Dad, chill out! I am just going to take some of the things I like, such as compassion and meditation; I am not going to follow the whole book!"

This is a guide for first-time mothers who stay at home in the first year of their baby's life. And while I am not comparing this book with a whole work on religion, I am asking you to not take this book too seriously and, actually, to not take motherhood in general too seriously. Don't expect everything to be perfect or that you are going to be the perfect mom that you always hoped you were going to be. Don't put too much pressure on yourself. In this guide, there might be chapters, subjects, or sections that you won't need or don't agree with, and that is absolutely fine.

I am not a celebrity. I am not a super chef (I learned how to cook when my baby started solids). I don't have one million followers on Instagram. I am not the former CEO of a successful company. I don't have a nanny and my parents do not live close by. I know that having a baby does not make me an expert. As I did not have a clue about babies before having one, I read all the books that you can imagine when I was pregnant. I considered all of them very useful and felt prepared to care for my baby but, after having the baby, I could not find any books to help me take care of myself. So, I started reading books and listening to audiobooks on a variety of subjects that I was interested in.

I became fascinated with topics such as habits and productivity and read books on these subjects from Charles Duhigg, Brian Tracy, Laura Vanderkam, and Arianna Huffington. I read books about the French approach to parenthood from Pamela Druckerman and their approach to beauty, skincare, and style from Mathilde Thomas and Jennifer L. Scott. Later in my reading, I "moved" to South Korea for more tips on a regimen for glowing skin, and I learned the anti-aging power of foods, herbs, and oils in skincare from Roxy Dillon in her book *Bio-Young*. I took style tips from Rachel Zoe's website and books. I was inspired by *Big Magic* from Elizabeth Gilbert and self-improvement authors like Jen Sincero, James Altucher, and Shauna Niequist. I learned about grit with Dr. Angela Duckworth and how to activate my brain from Dr. Wendy Suzuki. I laughed and consoled myself with the hilarious British moms' books of Katie Kirby and Sarah Turner. I read the famous *Happiness Project* by Gretchen Rubin and, without realizing, I started to create mine. Lastly, I craved spiritual guidance and began following the trails of the late Dr. Wayne Dyer, Mastin Kipp, and the brilliant Gabby Bernstein. I was like a sponge, and I read many more books than I can list here, but I do mention them at the end of this book. Also during my first year as a mom, I had the chance to talk to top dermatologists, nutritionists, fitness instructors, makeup artists, and, most importantly, to a lot of new moms who were going through the same experience as me.

So here you go: I am a mother who enjoys reading, asking a lot of questions, and finding out about healthy lifestyles and beauty, and I want to share my experiences and my knowledge with other new moms who may be feeling left without a resource on self-care. I had worked since I was 20 years old and now that I was in my mid-30s, I really wanted to enjoy this stay-at-home mom thing, which everyone (including my mom!) said was going to be so terrible. My hope is that you might learn from, get inspired by, find comfort in, disagree with, or at least laugh at the mommy experiences in this book.

Culturally, we have come to accept that once a baby is born, the focus should be on the baby. However, you won't find any advice about your baby in this book. (OK, maybe a little. Sorry, I couldn't help it!) This book is for you. At the end of the day, a happy mom equals a happy baby! I hope you enjoy this book and the wonderful, sweet, exhausting, challenging, humbling, messy (literally!), and rewarding ride that is motherhood.

Enjoy!
Sara Gaviria

Introduction

There are so many books about how to care for your baby, but I could hardly find a book about how to care for myself as a new mom. The only advice was "Sleep when the baby sleeps." Is that even realistic?

I read so many books to prepare for my baby, and I had the perfect birth plan—an empowering, quick, calm, natural birth—just like my close friend had. She recommended hypnobirthing, a type of childbirth that uses self-hypnosis techniques to combat fear and pain. I hired a doula. I even chose the song I wanted to play at the moment of birth: Pachelbel's "Canon in D," my wedding song.

When I was twelve days overdue, my doctor wanted to induce. I did not want to do this and was relieved when my water broke the day before I was scheduled for the induction. I was so happy that everything was, once again, going according to my plan. Then I was in labor without an epidural for twelve hours. It was painful, and I felt like it would never end, but I got through it, thanks to my doula and my husband. My mother struggled with seeing me in such pain and kept insisting that I have an epidural. I asked my husband (not in a very kind way) to take her out of the room. Yes, that's right. I kicked my own mother out of the delivery room!

After pushing for three hours with no progress, the doctor said the baby needed to be delivered by vacuum or C-section. There was no chance in hell that I was going to allow the vacuum, but the C-section sounded like a hot-stone massage by the beach at the Four Seasons in Maui. I am being very specific because I had my honeymoon there and that massage was one of the most indulgent experiences of my life. That is how good a C-section sounded after twelve hours of labor. So, I agreed. My doula suggested I try once more, but I was done. I had given all I had.

When I heard about successful birth stories without any complications, it was always "I was at work and two hours later I had the baby in my arms." or "I had a natural delivery and I felt so connected with the baby, it didn't even hurt." "I didn't feel anything with the epidural and the next thing I knew, there was my baby." I really wish I had that story. I was kind of brainwashed about the hypno-birthing thing, and I'd read so many books with success stories that I thought I was going to be one too. When I ran my first half marathon at age 30, I had a goal of running it in less than two hours. I had never run a mile in my life. I trained hard for four months and ran it in 1:59:12. If I could do a half marathon, of course I was going to rock this labor thing. I just needed to prepare myself like I had for the half marathon. I took a course. I read three books. I listened to my audio every night. I even had belly dancing lessons to apply when I was in labor. Which, of course, is the last thing you want to do when you are having real frickin' contractions.

Things did not go as I planned, and this is lesson number one on motherhood—nothing ever goes as planned! My main goals after delivery were to have a healthy and happy baby and get my body back. I was focused on my appearance. I wanted a flat stomach and I wanted to keep my hair (please, please hair, don't fall out!). What I did not know is that, in addition to discovering the most unconditional and out-of-this-world love for my baby, that everyone told me I was going to feel, I was also about to rediscover myself. I would begin to think about what really makes me happy and be very mindful of my free time. (Believe it or not, you will have free time.) I would read non-stop, look after myself, and try to understand the new dynamics in my relationship with my husband. I would get healthier, become a decent cook for my baby, declutter my house, reinvent my look, and be inspired to have self-discipline, enjoy nature, dare greatly, value every day, and make new friends at age 36.

Join me on the journey.

Part One
First Month

Welcome Home!

The hospital allowed me to stay for four days, the last day until 4 p.m. and I left at 3:55 p.m. I was so happy to be completely taken care of, but I was also excited to come home with my baby. I made a video of our arrival (I recommend doing that; it is such a nice memory.) The baby slept almost the whole afternoon, waking up only to be fed. But at about 8:00 p.m., he saw the unfamiliar house (I think) and completely freaked out. He started crying hysterically, and we had no idea what to do. I went to the washing machine to grab a clean blanket and when I went back to my room, I saw my husband shirtless, skin-to-skin with our son. I am the mom! I am supposed to do that. Then I went to his nursery and my mom was organizing my baby clothes. I yelled, "I am the mom and you two are treating me like I'm only a milk machine!" And there you go, I'd had my first mommy breakdown. Many other things happened over the first days with the baby at home. My baby's poo splashing spectacularly on the wall of his perfect nursery on Mother's Day, just two weeks after he was born, was another first-month highlight.

You have probably heard that you should take advantage of family and friends who live close by. This is great advice. It helps with the stress levels, even if it's just for a couple of hours. They can be valuable in helping keep you sane.

Welcome Home!

It was great to have my mom for those two weeks. She looked after me so well. She is the second of my Colombian grandma's ten children, so she knows a thing or two about babies. Below are some of the things that she did for me that were helpful. Be ready for these Colombian traditions.

Hot Chocolate. According to our Colombian grandmas, the uterus has "colds" after the delivery and your mission is to get it "hot" again. The way to do it is with hot chocolate. They also believed that this would help with milk production and aid in weight loss, as it shrinks your uterus quicker. I had it every single day in the morning for the first 40 days. My mom had a very peculiar way to make it, but it tasted much better than when I made it: mix two spoons of the chocolate (check the ingredients to make sure there is no high-fructose corn syrup) or raw cacao powder with a cup of cold non-dairy plant milk in a blender. (If you are using raw cacao powder, which I highly recommend, avoid dairy, as it will prevent anti-oxidant absorption.) Add a cinnamon stick and put it in the microwave for one minute. Take out the cinnamon stick and there you go! If you don't want to use a blender, mix all the ingredients in a large saucepan and bring to a boil. Discard the cinnamon stick and whisk ingredients until they become frothy. Remove from heat and serve hot and have it in the morning. Another benefit of cacao is it boosts brain levels of serotonin, the feel-good brain chemical that provides a feeling of well-being and enhances energy, which is exactly what you need! (More about cacao in the natural drinks section.)

Cinnamon. Cinnamon has amazing healing properties. It keeps glucose levels stable, helps digestion, has antioxidant powers, and boosts the immune system. It is also a great sugar replacement. My mom gave me cinnamon water. According to my grandmother, if you're breastfeeding, it helps prevent colic. Just hot water with one cinnamon stick will do the trick. I prefer organic cinnamon sticks and drinking it in the morning. I can tell you that my baby boy was easy and calm; he never had colic. Perhaps I was lucky, but all my aunties back in Colombia attribute it to my cinnamon drink.

Remember, these are just Colombian grandma's tales or, as my husband says, "Colombian witches" tales, but I feel that they really worked for me. Plus, hot chocolate and cinnamon water are delicious!

How Colombian Abuelas (grandmothers) Lived Their Cuarentena

After my abuela gave birth to each one of her babies, she entered a period called "cuarentena," as many other new mothers in Colombia did. It was a 40-day process that mothers used to help them recover and slowly reincorporate to their lives. Once they returned from the hospital, or after giving birth to their babies at home, they had to be lying down as much as they could for 40 days to let their uterus recover.

They believed this 40-day indigenous ritual would help them get their bodies back in shape more easily and help prevent illnesses that could affect them and their newborns. On the "cuarentena," new mothers were not to do any hard work; including sweeping, mopping, ironing, heavy lifting, washing clothes, using knives, or even cooking. They believed that their bodies needed rest from these efforts, and also avoided exposing themselves to extreme hot and cold temperatures. The consequences of avoiding these recommendations were back pain, bleeding, hip and waist pain, and kidney failure. During these 40 days, friends and relatives would help with the household chores. The father was asked to take the baby to any medical appointments.

In this century, most of us try to get back to our normal lives in a matter of days postpartum, but my grandma and many others back then in Colombia were not allowed to even get out of bed or take a shower!

Indigenous doctors in Latin America believed that during pregnancy a woman goes through a heating process to create the miracle of life. Like a bun in the oven, literally! An oven that stays on for nine months. When giving birth, a woman's uterus expands and expels the baby, the placenta, blood, and other tissue. They believed that giving birth makes us lose a significant amount of energy and exposes us to receiving cold in our boiling bodies, disrupting our temperature balance.

Back then, a new mother's head would be covered to keep her from catching cold and prevent headaches, spasms, fever, bone pain, cramps, and even psychosis. That is why the "cuarentena" was so important for my grandmother and other women of her time.

A mentioned earlier, hot chocolate was highly recommended for new moms. This hot beverage was to be consumed every day for 40 days postpartum. They believed when they drank it, that their bodies would sweat out the coldness they caught during the delivery.

They also believed that consuming hen soup every day (one hen per day!) would help the new mother recover her strength and improve her milk production. On the 40th day, she was to eat a chicken soup made of an entire chicken and take a vaginal steam to eliminate the "colds" from her uterus.

Below is a sample of what they used to recommend for a "cuarentena" after giving birth:

* **Days 1–7:** A new mother should stay home and not leave the house at all. She can only clean herself with hot, damp herbal-infused towels. Water by nature is cold, and that is why a new mother is not allowed to shower. She should not eat cold fruits or vegetables, or consume cold drinks.

* **Days 8–21:** She can start showering with hot water every two days. No cold foods, including fruits and vegetables.

* **Days 22–39:** She can start going outside, but only between 9:00 a.m. and 4:00 p.m., and she must be covered to avoid cold temperatures. She can start eating normally, with the exception of cold foods. She can shower regularly.

* **Day 40:** Consume hen soup and take vaginal steam (explained below).

After I gave birth, my mom sent me a reminder on my 40th day. (I didn't even know which day it was.) She sent me a very detailed text message on how to bathe and do the herbal vaginal steam. I was to boil water for fifteen minutes with chamomile, lemon, eucalyptus, mint, peppermint, basil, and gardenia petals. Then I had to pour that into a bowl and carefully squat or sit over it to let the steam go up into my vaginal opening. Traditionally, vaginal steaming was used for new mothers in Colombia to remove blood clots that were still there from giving birth, and during the "cuarentena" to help heal the uterus, take the cold out of her body, ease pain, and cleanse impurities from their body.

After reading that text, as I held my phone in one hand and my crying baby in the other, I replied with a blunt: "Are you serious?" At the time, the only thing I cared about was finding a diaper rash cream that actually worked. I didn't have time to buy all these herbs, boil them, and then squat over a bowl! And no, I didn't do it.

I must say though, that neither my mother nor her four sisters followed the "cuarentena" recommendations, and all had their uterus removed at some point in their lives for various medical reasons. Meanwhile, my grandma, at age 82 and after delivering 10 babies, still has her uterus. Coincidence?

Common Conditions after Delivery

Constipation

Normally, bowel movements will resume within the first few days following your baby's birth. If you experience postpartum constipation, here are a few suggestions:

* Start your day with some hot water with lemon and drink at least eight to ten large glasses of water a day at room temperature.

* Eat prunes (juice counts, too). They are a natural mild laxative. Raisins, figs, and or dried apricots mixed with some nuts are also a good idea.

* Eat crunchy fresh fruits and vegetables, leaving the skins intact.

* Try whole-grain cereals, breads, brown rice, lentils, and beans.

* Splash a little olive oil on your fish, chicken, and pasta.

* Move around several times a day (even at a slow pace).

* Avoid white rice and white bread, chocolate and bananas.

* Consult with your doctor if you do not have a bowel

movement by the third or fourth day after giving birth. You need a prescription for a safe, effective stool softener and/or a laxative.

Hemorrhoids

Hemorrhoids are swollen veins in the rectal area. They can range from simply itchy to absolutely painful and may even cause rectal bleeding, especially when you do have a bowel movement.

For short-term relief, you can choose from many OTC hemorrhoid creams, ointments, suppositories, or spray. You can also soak in a sitz bath. Just fill a basin with warm water and sit in it two to four times a day. You can also use cold packs on the area. If you don't have a cold pack, put some ice in a plastic bag, cover with a thin cloth, and place it over the affected area for 10 to 20 minutes at a time. There is also a natural treatment popular in Colombia that can be very effective to help relieve hemorrhoids: avocado seeds. You read right! Adding them to a sitz bath can help eliminate the annoying symptoms of hemorrhoids in a short time. They can also help the swelling go down. Here's what you'll need:

Sitz Bath with Avocado Seeds

3 avocado seeds
4 liters of water
2 tablespoons of baking soda

Peel the avocado seeds until they are white and then cut them into four pieces and boil for 25 minutes. Add the baking soda and boil 5 more minutes then remove from heat. Let it cool to warm; use half a liter for the sitz bath. Stay seated for 15 minutes or until the water cools completely. When the remaining batch of water gets to room temperature, place it in a covered container and store it in the fridge. You can take the bath two to four times a day. You should feel great relief from the first one and in the following days, the hemorrhoids should be noticeably less swollen.

Vaginal Bleeding

Whether you delivered vaginally or by C-section, you will experience post-partum discharge. During the first week, the bleeding will be bright red with a few small clots and the flow will be similar to a menstrual period. Over the first two to six weeks following birth, the color will change from bright red to pinkish brown, and then fade to cream or white. The bleeding usually stops in three to six weeks. At home, continue to use sanitary pads. Do not use tampons, as this can cause infection of your healing uterus.

Report to your doctor any heavy vaginal bleeding (soaking more than one pad per hour), large clots, a bleeding that stays bright red past the first week, a foul odor, or unusual abdominal pain or tenderness.

No one told me about...

You now know all the things that can happen to your body after giving birth—constipation, breast engorgement, hemor-rhoids—but what about night sweats? You may want to keep plenty of clean PJs and a blanket for when you are cold and try to change your sheets every day. Great! As If you didn't already have enough laundry to do! Postpartum sweating is due to your hormones readjusting to you not being pregnant anymore. Call your doctor if you have a temperature of 100.4 or higher, as that can indicate an infection.

Breastfeeding

Whether or not to breastfeed is such a personal choice, but the American Pediatric Association recommends breastfeeding up to at least one year. I did it for 13 months and had enough milk to feed a small country! (Must be that hot chocolate!)

Fortunately, breastfeeding came very naturally to me in the beginning. Even though I had a C-section and my husband was the one to have first contact with the baby, my son latched on straight away when he was put on my chest. It felt amazing! I did not have any problems or pain. I was still high on happiness, exhaustion, and . . . anesthesia.

The third day, however, was a very different experience. When the nurse woke me up and said it was time to nurse, my nipples were sore and peeling, and one was almost black. Almost in tears, I begged to give him a bottle. Thankfully, the nurse refused. Our conversation went something like this:

Me: "I am in so much pain."

Nurse: (Checking her chart) "Actually, you have not had your medicine for pain for the last 12 hours."

Me: (Looking very shocked and annoyed) "Why?"

Nurse: (Looking very confused) "It says . . . you have not requested it."

Me: (High tone.) "Um, I was in labor without an epidural for 12 hours (high pitch here) followed by a lovely C-section. How on earth am I going to remember when I have to take my pills?"

Nurse: (Looking embarrassed.) "OK, Mrs. Gaviria, do you want your medicine every four or six hours?"

Me: "Four."

Nurse: "One dose or two?"

Me: "Two."

Nurse: "Level of pain from 1 to 10?"

Me: "21."

Then I had a visit from the lactation consultant. When she saw me, she made a face of such horror that I started crying. If the lactation consultant who sees many sore and swollen breasts was surprised, this meant I was in trouble. She asked if I had ever heard of a nipple shield. Of course I hadn't, but it turned out to be the best thing for me. A nipple shield is a nipple-shaped sheath that is worn over the areola and nipple during breast-feeding. They are made of soft, thin, flexible silicone and have holes at the end of the nipple section to allow the breast milk to pass through.

When I have a friend tell me excitedly that she is pregnant, the first thing I say is, "You have to buy the nipple shield!" If it weren't for this heaven-sent gadget, I don't think I would have breastfed.

The nipple shield is a win-win—the baby feeds better and you don't have irritated nipples. Some books and lactation consultants are against nipple shields for the first few days or weeks, because they worry it will interfere with latching on, but my nipples were already sore and peeling, and I had a tiny piranha biting them every two hours. In my case, I had to buy the shields.

If you do use them, make sure to buy several, as they are so small and transparent that they easily get lost in your nursing pillow, blankets, bed, and glider. I lost one at the hospital and asked my husband to buy me one from the hospital store. He commented that he had just bought me one. I gave him a stern look and told him to go and buy me another one! I refused to nurse without one. Also, make sure they are clean. I used them starting on the third day and I stopped using them after a month or two. Of course, there are moms who don't need them or just need them for a couple of days or weeks, but if you have very sore nipples, this can be a great solution.

When breastfeeding, remember to eat frequent snacks and meals. As Luiza DeSouza says in her book *Eat Play Sleep* (which I strongly recommend for the first three months), "When you were pregnant, your body stored extra calories that are now used to produce breast milk. Therefore, in the initial months of breastfeeding, your "yield"—how much and what kind of milk you produce—is not dependent on what you eat. Still, if your diet is inadequate—if you do not consume enough proteins, fats, and carbohydrates or drink enough water—your body will use those stored calories quickly. You will feel irritated. Not only will that affect your milk production, but you also might become depressed."

Breastfeeding 911

If your milk supply is low, these can help you.

* Drinking plenty of water
* Sleep (when you can!)
* Organic Mother's Milk Tea by Traditional Medicinals
* Organic Milkmaid Tea by Earth Mama Angel Baby Organic
* Fenugreek Pills Organically Grown by Solaray
* Brewer's Yeast Powder by Innovative Kal Quality. (Mix with water, tea, smoothie, or juice)
* Lactation Cookies by Milkmakers

Lactation Cookie Recipe

This dairy-free recipe has no refined sugar and will help boost/maintain your milk supply. The brewer's yeast is the active ingredient that makes this a "lactation" cookie. The oats and flax seed are great for milk production, too, and the dark chocolate, bananas, and peanut butter will help mask the bitter taste of the yeast. You can make them or ask a lovely person from your family or group of friends to make them for you. As the author of this recipe suggests, keep an already baked batch in the freezer and just pop a few in the toaster oven to reheat whenever you want an easy snack or a quick, one-handed breakfast. They taste really good, but don't eat them all at once! Two per day will be enough for your milk supply. If this is too much to handle, just buy the cookie mix from Milkmakers (available on Amazon) or yummymummycookies.com.

Ingredients

3 large, ripe bananas, well mashed (about 1½ cups)

1 teaspoon vanilla extract

½ cup coconut oil, warmed to a liquid state

¼ cup peanut butter or almond butter

3 cups rolled oats

⅔ cup almond meal or flour

3 tablespoons ground flax seed

4 tablespoons reduced bitterness brewer's yeast

½ teaspoon Kosher salt

½ teaspoon cinnamon

1 teaspoon baking powder

1½ cups) chocolate chips or dark chocolate bar chopped (optional)

For extra sweetness and to reduce the flavor of the yeast, double the vanilla and the cinnamon and/or add one tablespoon of brown sugar or agave.

Instructions

1. Preheat oven to 350 degrees, racks in the top third.

2. In a large bowl combine the bananas, vanilla extract, coconut oil, and peanut butter. Set aside. In another bowl, whisk together the oats, almond meal, flax seed, brewer's yeast, salt, cinnamon, and baking powder.

3. Add the dry ingredients to the wet ingredients and stir until combined.

Fold in the chocolate chips/chunks. The dough will be a bit looser than a standard cookie dough. Drop dollops of the dough, each about 2 table-spoons in size, an inch apart, onto a parchment-lined baking sheet (the cookies won't spread so they can be placed pretty close together).

4. Bake for 16 to 18 minutes, until the oats are toasty. Check them about three quarters of the way through baking time to make sure the bottoms don't burn.

RECIPE SOURCE: LICKMYSPOON.COM

Wine, anyone?

The American Academy of Pediatrics (AAP) states that nursing mothers can have an occasional alcoholic drink (the equivalent of a 12-ounce beer, 4-ounce glass of wine, or ounce of hard liquor) but that she should wait at least two hours per drink before breastfeeding. I did not drink while I was breastfeeding my baby. It might sound extreme, but not having to deal with pumping milk, storing milk and sterilizing bottles was better than a glass of wine. (I absolutely hated pumping, everything about it, even the sound!)

When you drink, about 2 percent of the alcohol you consume will enter your bloodstream and breast milk. However, since everyone metab-olizes alcohol differently, the amount of time it takes for the alcohol in breast milk to metabolize also varies. Metabolism depends on many factors, including body weight, type of alcohol consumed, and food intake. To find out when the alcohol has really left the breast milk, you can use a Milkscreen test kit. UpSpring Baby Milkscreen for breastfeeding is recom-mended by pediatricians and lactation consultants.

Did you know...

75 percent of moms produce more milk from their right breast? (I am part of this percentage!) Even though you produce more milk from one breast, always attempt to switch and feed from

each breast to avoid looking "uneven." It happened to me in the last months of breastfeeding, and was not fun wearing a swimsuit or tight tops.

Breastfeeding saves a family $2,000 to $4,000 annually. According to *The Longevity Book* by Cameron Diaz, each childbirth reduces a woman's risk of developing breast cancer by 7 percent. Every year of breastfeeding reduces the risk of breast cancer by 4 percent, and every month of breastfeeding reduces the risk of ovarian cancer by 2 percent. This may be because lactation stops ovulation, reducing levels of estrogen and progesterone, which are major risk factors for breast cancer. Lactation also changes how breast cells behave, making them less likely to develop into a breast cancer cells.

Weaning your baby

It is your decision when to wean your baby. Don't feel bad if you do it earlier than others or if you breastfeed more than a year.

Just substitute one nursing session at a time for a sippy cup of organic whole milk if your baby is over 12 months, or formula if he is younger than 12 months. I did it when my son was 13 months old. The first session that I substituted was lunchtime. After three days of that, I substituted the morning one as well, so that we were down to two breastfeedings a day—one before nap and one before bed. After two weeks, I was nursing at bedtime only. Then I cut the duration of the session. At the beginning, I nursed for ten minutes, then eight, six, and so on until, on the last day, I nursed for only two minutes. By this time, my son was ready to quit and I didn't experience any engorgement.

Reruns

If you are planning on watching TV, this is the time! You will spend so much time nursing, pumping, and having the baby sleeping in your arms.

One of the best things I did was move my amazing glider, which looked perfect in my nursery, to the living room. I caught up on my favorite reality TV shows and Netflix series. Seriously, there is no shame. If you want to see reruns of your favorite TV show while you are feeding your baby, go ahead—this is the time! You just grew and delivered a human being; you are entitled to reality TV or whatever your guilty pleasure is. Actually, this could be the only thing keeping you sane. You will look forward to your 40-minute feeding so you can find out why no one liked the Red Wedding episode of *Game of Thrones*. Just turn down the volume a bit and make sure that the TV is not directly facing your baby.

The Important Part of Breastfeeding is Feeding

The breastfeeding support groups at some hospitals are great. I went to Sharp in San Diego, and they were very helpful when I had questions. These groups are devised to help mothers and babies with the challenges of breastfeeding. They weigh your baby before and after feeding and give you new ideas and techniques to try to improve your breastfeeding success at home. Usually, this support group is free, and registration is not required. Fathers are also welcome. I know when you have a newborn, you are sleep-deprived and overwhelmed, the last thing you want to do is get ready and go to a room full of strangers with their breasts out, but if you are having trouble breastfeeding, it is absolutely worth it. All the moms and dads are only focused on their own babies, and the lactation consultants are very gentle and encouraging. Also, you can also ask questions regarding your baby apart from breastfeeding. Better yet, it's not only for newborns; if your baby is older and you still have questions, you can go. I went to my first session when my baby was four months old and he was having reflux problems. I regretted not going earlier.

If you've tried the teas, the cookies, and the group, and you still cannot breastfeed, here's some advice: If you don't produce enough milk, do not stress; just use both bottle and breast or give your baby formula. Low milk production is not uncommon among new mothers. I know that it is easier said than done, but know that you are doing the right thing by recognizing you need to supplement your baby. Also, be aware that your stress will not help the baby while cuddling and during skin-to-skin contact. The most important part of breastfeeding is feeding. Just relax and move on to the important job of caring for your baby as best you can, and remember to enjoy every single moment of their development.

Me, My Baby, And My Waist Trainer

The first month, just focus on your baby and your recovery. Don't weigh yourself or try to fit into your old clothes. Enjoy your baby, go for short, easy walks, and eat healthily If you want to treat yourself once in a while, do it, just don't *overdo* it. Drink water, have lots of fresh fruits and vegetables, and eat protein twice a day. This is very important for your recovery, for your milk supply if you are breastfeeding, and for weight loss. Try to eat as healthily as you can during this time you're unable to exercise intensively.

This month do something nice for yourself. Go for a manicure, pedicure, haircut, or color touch-up. (I don't recommend doing anything drastic with your haircut or color, though. You may not be mentally ready for a full makeover, as you already have a new human being in your home; you do not need any other drastic changes. If you want to be adventurous, try a new nail polish color.) Go have a cup of coffee alone to catch up on messages, or chat with a dear friend. And take as many photos as you can of your angel. Everyone says the same, but it is so true. It goes so fast!

For the first 4-8 weeks, just focus on recovering and acclimating to your new life as a mother: sleep when you can and do not worry about your husband, your visitors, your hair, or the house. If you're comfortable going out three days after the delivery, go ahead. If not, stay at home. If there are people who want to see you and you don't feel like it, it is OK. They will understand. Leave the house looking lovely or a mess, whichever makes you feel better.

I remember making a big effort on my first going-out with my husband and the baby for brunch—putting makeup on, blow drying my hair, and wearing flat boots and a nice jacket. I wanted desperately to feel like my old self again. But now when I see new mommies in restaurants having brunch with their partners and babies, their hair pulled back and no makeup, just that mommy glow and comfy clothes—I think they look stunning! They may have tired eyes, but their genuine and peaceful smiles show that they don't care about any of that. They are solely focused on their babies, and that is true beauty.

The only two concerns you should have for the first months are taking care of yourself and your baby, but that doesn't mean we have to completely let ourselves go. Something that helped me and I do recommend is wearing a waist trainer. Yes, it can be uncomfortable, but it actually helps you to suck it in! I only took it off at bedtime (I could not sleep with it on!). Of course, there will be days that you do not want to wear it or you won't have time to put it on, but please try to wear it as much as possible. I did not put it on straight after my delivery, but I started wearing it after week two and continued using it for the next three months. It helps with your posture and you will look slimmer, which can boost your self-confidence postpartum. In fact, Jessica Alba admitted to *Net-a-Porter's The Edit Magazine back in 2013* that she used a corset to get her pre-baby body back after both of her pregnancies, "I wore a double corset day and night for three months," she told the magazine. "It was brutal; it's not for everyone." However, she went on to say it was "sweaty but worth it."

I recommend Bellefit and Camellias Women's Latex Waist Trainer Corset, both available at Amazon. (What's not available at Amazon?) Make sure that it has adjustable hooks so you can make it tight, but bearable. There has been a bit of controversy about the effectiveness of the waist trainer but after having a baby, they definitely help you get a flat stomach. In Colombia, this is considered a must after giving birth. Once you get where you want to be, just forget about it. I never wore mine again.

Finally, for the first month, make time to rest and don't be too hard on yourself. Take at least two weeks before you start trying to catch up and even longer if you had a C-section. This stage of motherhood lasts a very short time; remember to enjoy it!

When my son was a newborn and I took him to the park or a coffee shop, people would look at him and say, "Oh, I don't even remember when mine was that little." It was a reminder for me to enjoy every moment; the days may be long, but the years are short.

First Comes Love, Then Comes C-Section

My C-section took me by surprise. I never thought I would have one. Every time a friend would bring up that she'd had a C-section or was going to have one, I thought to myself very confidently, "That is not going to happen to me."

At first, it didn't seem like a big deal. After having my C-section, I was still able to have skin-to-skin contact with my baby, and he started to latch straight away. I was tired but happy and very aware of everything. When they took me to my room, I wasn't in pain. I was so happy my baby was healthy that I didn't think of anything else. I saw some tubes and I felt some compression on my legs, but I didn't think it was a big deal. The next morning, the doctor checked on me and asked a lot of questions about how I was feeling. I thought this was odd, but then the nurse said, "You just had surgery," and that is when it hit me. The pain that I felt after being without medication for 12 hours also made me more aware of what I had just gone through. I had read every single thing I could find about pregnancy, but about C-sections, I did not have a clue. It wasn't until afterwards that I realized I had gone through a major surgery.

It took me a while to recover mentally from my unexpected C-section. I had days that it was the only thing I could think of and I didn't feel I could share it with anyone. My mom and my sister never thought that I could have a natural birth, so I was afraid of the "I told you so." With my friends, I had been on my high-horse, telling them how hypnosis at night was really working, and that I would only have to think about how each contraction was going to get me closer to my baby. I did not want them to make fun of me. I did not want the judgmental looks and them thinking, "I knew you couldn't do it." I could not share it with my husband, either, because he could not see what the big deal was and did not want to talk about it. (Have I mentioned that my husband is British?) Now that time has passed, I think the judgment I feared was mostly in my mind.

During my weeks of recovery, even though I felt good and energetic, there was a funny pain down there. I wondered if I was OK, if they had put everything back properly. Would I ever feel like my old self again? Would I be able to bend and do abs? I thought that sensation was going to stay with me forever.

I wanted to talk to the doctor who had delivered my baby. I had so many questions, and I spent the whole morning before my six-week appointment preparing myself for the visit. In the end, I only saw his assistant and didn't get all my questions answered. When I left the appointment, I saw my doctor in his office and wanted to go in and ask him what I could have done to avoid a C-section. Did I have a C-section because I was trying for a natural birth or because my baby's head was large? (His head actually was larger than most. When I went to his 6 and 9- month check-up appointments his weight and height were usually average, but his head was always in the 80% percentile.) Most important, had I put my baby in danger? I was heading to my doctor's office and then I stopped because I was afraid to know the real truth. I left with not only my funny sensations down there, but with a feeling of defeat and uncertainty.

I know that there are worst things that could have happened. My baby was healthy and I had a good recovery. I was very grateful for that.

After months of feeling sad about my C-section, I talked to my sister. She asked why I cared so much what other people thought. *The most important thing is that my nephew is healthy. What's the big deal about having the baby out of your vagina? I actually think that's gross!* I couldn't help but laugh!

(Of course, my sister has no kids yet). She reminded me that it didn't really matter how he'd come into the world. The important thing was that he was healthy. This helped me feel better about how things had turned out.

Mothers shouldn't feel ashamed that things didn't go the way we felt they should have. Find someone that you trust and talk about your feelings. If you're really struggling to get through it, seek help. There are several support groups you can reach out to. The International Cesarean Awareness Network, Inc. (ICAN) is a nonprofit organization whose mission is to improve maternal-child health by providing support for cesarean recovery.

If the idea of sharing your birth story makes you anxious, afraid, or overwhelmed, look for individual counseling. A therapist who works with women's issues can help you to learn coping skills to manage your distress. You don't have to do it alone.

I had made a lovely and detailed album of my pregnancy, which arrived after my baby boy was born. In the beginning, I only looked at it a couple of times. It made me feel sad to see the photos where I looked so happy and healthy, thinking that everything was going to go according to my plan. One day, after reading books to my son, I saw the album and picked it up. I took a deep breath and started looking through it. I saw this amazing journey and decided not to let the C-section define my pregnancy, the arrival of my beautiful son or my first year as a mother. I'd had a healthy and perfect pregnancy and accept that everything happens for a reason, and that I'd had the best intentions in every decision I made and was grateful for all my blessings. Sometimes in life we may not get the answers we seek, we just accept it and move on.

For me, a straight talk with my sister, some meditation, and the passage of time were enough. I also read the book *Daring Greatly: How the Courage to be Vulnerable Transforms the Way We Live, Love, Parent and Lead* by Brené Brown and watched her TED talk *The Power of Vulnerability*. Both made me realize that being vulnerable it is not a weakness (like I always thought) but is actually the opposite and can become your biggest strength. According to Brown, *Daring Greatly* means having the courage to be vulnerable, to show up and be seen. To ask for what you need and talk about how you are feeling. To have the hard conversations. I understood that daring greatly really transforms the way we live. When we feel safe enough to show our vulnerability is when we become free and freedom is true happiness. Since I now embrace vulnerability, I am able to share this experience with you.

Brown also shares a quote by Theodore Roosevelt:

It is not the critic who counts; not the man who points out how the strong man stumbles, or where the doer of deeds could have done them better. The credit belongs to the man who is actually in the arena, whose face is marred by dust and sweat and blood; who strives valiantly; who errs, who comes short again and again, because there is no effort without error and shortcoming; but who does actually strive to do the deeds; who knows great enthusiasms, the great devotions; who spends himself in a worthy cause; who at the best knows in the end the triumph of high achievement, and who at the worst, if he fails, at least fails while daring greatly, so that his place shall never be with those cold and timid souls who neither know victory nor defeat.

Now when I think back to my natural birth plan, I take a deep breath and think . . . I gave it all that day and was afraid to show my disappointment when it didn't go as planned, so I protected myself from being vulnerable for fear of being judged. But, today, today I dare greatly! Exhale . . .

C-section kit

* **C-Section Recovery Postpartum Girdle.** Buy the size you were pre-pregnancy. It has three adjustments; you'll think it won't fit, but you'll get there. Otherwise, buy just one size up. Keep in mind that your bump will shrink quickly, and these girdles are not cheap! $90 average.
* **C Panty underwear**
* **Scar Cream BioCorneum.** Scientific studies show that silicone-based scar creams and silicone sheeting

are effective in reducing the risk of thick scars and can even help thin out existing scars. It is recommended by plastic surgeons and dermatologists and is the cream I personally used. It costs about $100 but lasts for quite a while. Strataderm is another great option and was highly recommended by my dermatologist.

* **Embrace Minimize**. This is a silicone sheet that protects and hydrates the scar site, helping to improve the appearance of old and new scars. One box contains three sheets and each sheet is designed to last an average of ten days. You can conveniently cut the sheet horizontally to get at least three from each sheet. The ultra-thin sheet is very easy to apply and water resistant. It reduces the itching, pain, and discomfort associated with scarring, and it works!

If your scar becomes raised and thickened (which is known as a hypertrophic or keloid scar) and if you have the budget for it, go to a cosmetic dermatologist. (Make sure that it is a doctor, not a cosmetologist.) The doctor can inject 5-FU to help break down the excessive collagen, causing the scar to get thinner. Do not use steroids for your injection. With steroids, there is a risk of the skin around the keloid scar shrinking, which is why it's recommended that you use it a maximum of two times. 5-FU is much better, and you can have the procedure as many times as needed. After your scar is flat, you can do a laser treatment, such as PDL (Pulsed Dye Laser) and IPL (Intense Pulsed Light), which can reduce the redness and sometimes, the size of the scar. It can take six to twelve months to see results. I am not going to tell you that the laser and the injection are painless, but it's done quickly—you'll survive.

That said, these treatments are not cheap; they can cost

from $200 to $400 per session. Start using the scar cream or sheets as soon as you have the green light from your doctor. Apply it two or three times a day, religiously. Set an alarm to apply the cream if needed or use the silicone sheets. Then every time you have a doctor appointment: OB, MD, dermatologist, even your dentist (I am only kidding on the last one) have him or her check your scar. Everyone's skin is different, but it should look thin and flat after a year.

Postpartum Depression

After giving birth, you will experience a wide range of feelings. This does not make you a bad mom. It makes you normal; it makes you human. Having a baby is a significant life stressor. When you bring a baby into your home, it is a major event that affects the entire family dynamic.

A 2015 study out of Germany showed that in the first year after childbirth there is a drop in happiness that is worse than that experienced during major negative life events such as divorce, unemployment, and even the death of a partner. (Personally, I think these findings are a bit extreme.)

But there is a big difference between "postpartum blues" or "baby blues" and postpartum depression.

Symptoms of Baby Blues

* Frustration or anger, irritability
* Feelings of tiredness, loss or mood swings
* Crying for no reason
* Trouble sleeping and eating
* Unsure of how to care for a baby

This is normal for 60 to 80 percent of women, and it will last for about two weeks. The hormonal changes following delivery, plus the stress and lack of sleep, can make domestic problems seem bigger than they would at any other time.

To ease the transition, look for help with the baby so you can get some rest. For some women these feelings go away easily, but if that is not your case, talk with your partner, a friend, or a family member. Exercise is also beneficial. As you are still recovering, go for an easy walk with your baby or on your own. Some fresh air and physical activity will help you feel better. Being outdoors gives you the benefit of natural light therapy If you find some greenery, even better. A study from Stanford University found that people who walked for 90 minutes in a natural setting showed lower levels of rumination (dwelling on the negative thoughts) than those who walked in an urban area.

Lauren Smith Brody suggests in her book *The Fifth Trimester* that you keep asking yourself "What do I need right now?" She says asking this question "is part of our creativity and intelligence as a parent. It's a strength, not a weakness." Try it: what do you need right now? Perhaps you need a long, hot shower or to talk to your mom on the phone while you eat a piece of chocolate cake. Maybe you need to go for a walk on your own or you need your husband to come home earlier from work to help you out. I'm being serious. When my son was three weeks old, I once made my husband come home at noon because I was exhausted. You could ask your best friend to help you with grocery shopping, talk to another new mom, buy a different nursing bra, get help with cleaning the house, have your husband do the insurance paperwork, make a doctor's appointment (for you!), watch one hour of reality TV with no interruptions, order your favorite takeout, or get a manicure with hand massage included. When we stay at home with our babies and don't have career responsibilities, family members and friends often expect that we can easily adapt to our new role and handle it alone without any support. This simply is not true. Think about what you need and ask for it. And this not only goes for the first month, make this a practice of ongoing self-care. Perhaps if you ask yourself this question on a daily basis and take action, you won't end up with a load of bundled-up emotions later. If the "blues" do not seem to go away two to three weeks after delivery or feelings become more intense, you could be experiencing postpartum depression.

Symptoms of Postpartum Depression

* Intense and persistent feelings of sadness, anxiety, guilt, or despair

* Change in appetite (overeating or no eating) and insomnia

* Inability to perform daily tasks or lack of interest in nearly all activity

* Experiencing little satisfaction and enjoyment with motherhood

* No desire to be with your baby

* Thoughts of harming yourself or your baby

What the Numbers Show

Depression is the leading cause of disease-related disability in women around the world. More women suffer from mental illness during and after pregnancy than those that develop gestational diabetes, pre-eclampsia, or go into preterm labor.

According to the Centers for Disease Control and Prevention, 1 in 9 women experience symptoms of postpartum depression. It can occur up to one year post-childbirth and affects about 600,000 women in the U.S. each year. Unfortunately, only 15 percent of women with postpartum depression ever receive professional treatment.

According to the U.S. Preventive Services Task Force, pregnant women and new mothers need more attention when it comes to screening for depression. Evidence shows that they can be accurately diagnosed and successfully treated, which is important because untreated depression harms not only the mother, but her child as well. And studies have shown that babies and toddlers with depressed moms are subject to a lot of problems.

They may be more difficult to console and less likely to interact and may even have more sleep problems.

If you or a member of your family suspect that you are experiencing postpartum depression, please speak up and know that you're not alone. It does not discriminate. Public figures such as Gwyneth Paltrow, Hayden Panettiere, Brooke Shields, Alanis Morissette, and Drew Barrymore have all suffered from this. There needs to be more discussion about postpartum depression. Call your healthcare provider and ask for help. By reaching out, you're already taking a crucial step for your health and the health of your baby.

What You Can Do

There are a lot of treatments for postpartum depression: participating in a support group, talk therapy, medication, or in extreme cases, hospitalization. About 90 percent of women who have postpartum depression can be treated successfully with medication or a combination of medication and psychotherapy.

Talk Therapy

New mothers who are reluctant to take medications during pregnancy or while breastfeeding might find that they benefit from the following therapies:

* **Cognitive Behavioral Therapy.** CBT has you flip back through your thinking and pull out your most worrisome thoughts. The idea is to bring the problem back into perspective so you can do something about it and move on. On the behavioral side, CBT gets you to gradually do things you may be leery of.

* **Mindfulness Based Cognitive Therapy.** Offers the added benefit of teaching mindfulness and meditation, which can help women manage the intense symptoms of anxiety and depression. (We will talk more about meditation and its benefits in chapter 4.)

Exercise

Research has shown that regular exercise can be more beneficial than certain antidepressant drugs. Christina Hibbert, author of *8 Keys to Mental Health*, says that exercise produces natural antidepressant effects. The author adds that exercise increases levels of feel-good chemicals such as serotonin, dopamine, and norepinephrine that people suffering from depression might be lacking. When you work out, areas of your brain are stimulated by these feel-good chemicals, giving you a positive feeling.

While you are recovering from postpartum depression, you will probably see an improvement from month to month. But be aware that your symptoms may return before a menstrual period, due to fluctuations in your hormones.

Admitting you're not well is difficult. Making yourself go to that therapy appointment, or attend that support group, or take that medication, is difficult. Don't be afraid to seek help. And please remember, the sooner you get help, the better it will be for both you and your baby. (And your partner and immediate family!) Having a baby should be one of the best experiences of your life, not one of the worst. With professional help, family support, and your determination, you can do it.

For resources on postpartum depression, check the Postpartum Stress Center at www.postpartumstress.com. You can also find good tips in the book *This Isn't What I Expected: Overcoming Postpartum Depression* by Karen R. Kleiman and Valerie D. Raskin.

Words of Wisdom for the First Month

If there is anything I learned right away about being a mom, it was not to judge. Every mom I know is doing this job the best way they can, and with so much love. No one deserves to be judged. If someone asks you how the baby scratched his face, what you do all day at home with the baby or mentions that you look tired and makes fun of your post-pregnancy hormones, be patient and try to not take it personally. They haven't walked your path or followed your journey. You are doing what is right for you and your family so you can be healthy and happy. Keep going. There is more to learn, as you will see in the next chapters.

Part Two
Healthy Eating & Exercise

When I was pregnant, I had a plan to lose the baby weight: one hour of cardio, one hour of weights and 30 minutes of abs. After having my baby, I realized I did not have the time or the energy! Most importantly, I began to recognize that in order to lose the weight, I also had to focus on healthy eating, choose the right combination of foods, and eat regularly. Once I got the OK from my doctor, I started to walk 20 to 30 minutes every day. Then I started enthusiastically running and doing weights. Did I say enthusiastically? Perhaps a little too enthusiastically. I injured my knees and I could not exercise for over a month. My husband recommended that I try spinning, as your knees have the support of the bike. Then I discovered yoga. Now, I practice it regularly and it is the exercise I enjoy. I started to lose the extra weight, my core became more toned, and the stretching helped me with the soreness of breastfeeding, made it easier for me to carry my baby (and the car seat!), and left me feeling relaxed. After all the craziness in the house, it is nice to have one calm hour for yourself. My husband recommended I try spinning, too, and when I was stuck and trying to lose those last few pounds, I felt that spinning really helped me. If you have the energy and a gym membership, this is a great way to burn the calories. But only if you enjoy it. Otherwise, look for options to work out at home. I will give some recommendations in this chapter.

If you are pregnant and reading this...

The best way to lose the weight after pregnancy is to not gain too much weight during the pregnancy. It sounds obvious, but it is so true. If you only gain the recommended 30 to 35 pounds, your body will bounce back easier and quicker. It's Mother Nature with a small push. Be careful with what you eat while pregnant. No extra calories are needed in the first trimester; 200 to 300 in second; and 500 in the third, during the rapid growth phase. Have a healthy breakfast (eggs, toast, oatmeal, and a smoothie); protein, veggies, and grains for lunch and dinner and healthy snacks. Drink plenty of water, do some exercise (walking counts) and if you are dying for a pizza, burger, brownie, or a crazy craving: apple pie with bacon on top, just have half and only once in a while. Think about your baby; your baby eats what you eat.

Month 1-2

The key to losing weight during the first months, as I mentioned in the previous chapter, is to eat well. You may not have the energy, the focus, or the time to work out during the first eight weeks. Eating well and walking worked for me. Do not diet, do not do any juicing or detox. Life with a newborn can be hard and stressful enough, the last thing you need is to put your body in starvation mode. You don't need to do any cardio either. When you have a baby, you are so tired and sleep deprived that the last thing you want to do is high-impact cardio that will stress your muscles and even joints more.

Be patient and remember it took time to put the weight on and it will take time to take it back off. The key to eating well is planning ahead and having healthy food choices on hand.

Keep Walking

It's easy to incorporate walking into your daily routine. You will need the fresh air, plus there will be times when the baby will only nap on the go! According to the Anxiety and Depression Association of America, walking triggers the body's relaxation response and helps to reduce stress. Even a quick ten-minute walk provides an immediate energy boost and improves your mood. Plus, it's good for your baby, too! Take advantage of your stroller rides and the fact that the baby is sleeping (hopefully!). Wear comfy shoes and don't forget your headphones. Once the baby is asleep, listen to fun or relaxing music, make calls (catch up with friends or your mom, make appointments and return phone calls you missed) or even better, listen to an audiobook. I downloaded the Overdrive app and it is wonderful; it has so many books available. Get the books that you always wanted to read or something fun and light. You will be so hooked on your books that you may find you walk longer and look forward to your next walk to continue with your book. In fact, exercisers using treadmills who listened to audiobooks went to the gym 51 percent more than usual in a study at the University of Pennsylvania. You could listen to a novel, podcasts, baby books, even self-improvement books. Don't ever underestimate them. There are so many things to take from those books, especially as a new mom.

For the first outings, you will probably only want to enjoy the fresh air or listen to chill music, but after a while, please take advantage of this precious time and do something for yourself. Reserve the audiobooks you want at your local library and then you can download them to your phone or the Overdrive app. You can also download podcasts that you are interested in or audiobooks from Amazon. It depends on your mood, but during my first months of being a mom, I read only self-improvement books. (I prefer to call them that instead of self-help.) I remember the first audiobook that I listened to after I had my baby was *The Life-Changing Magic of Tidying Up* by Marie Kondo and it helped me to organize my house and get rid of old stuff that I no longer needed. I also like reading books by inspiring women. It is encouraging to read about women who worked very hard to get where they are and learn about everything they had to overcome.

The extra mile...

Something that helped me with my recovery was to have the same route with my stroller. I did an extra block or even just an extra couple of steps every day. That kept me focused and motivated. When I was feeling better and a bit stronger (after ten weeks) I took a mat, put it in the stroller, and did ten minutes of abs or planks in the park while my baby was sleeping.

You already know what your baby needs. This is YOUR list of things you'll want for your walks:

Stroller

* A bottle of water with lemon

* A piece of fruit (banana or apple)

* A homemade coffee or smoothie (Try not to buy those more than once a week as a treat. You will save money and extra calories.)

* Headphones

* Sunblock

* Hand sanitizer

* A hat (I always leave mine in the stroller, so I don't forget it)

Always have your stroller ready for walks. Once the baby is in the stroller, you will be in a rush to leave if he starts crying.

Diaper bag

* One extra top (for you) in case your baby spits ups or vomits all over you. You'll only need it in extreme cases. Otherwise, just use a baby wipe. I only found out how effective a baby wipe can be after I had a baby. If they can clean up poop, they can clean anything!

* Nude lipstick (it will work as a lipstick and a blush when you can't find or don't have one; just do two swipes on each cheek and rub it in with your fingers)

* Hand sanitizer (I have loads and put one in almost each

pocket, as I usually lose or can't find one when I need it!)

* Mints

* Sunblock

* Headbands

* Ziploc bag with raw almonds. Best snack. It's healthy, doesn't go bad and is filling. Just be careful when your baby is older and starts curiously looking through your bag.

What To Drink?

Smoothies

This yummy recipe will help you to feel energetic in the morning and if you are breastfeeding, it will help with your milk supply, too. And please, don't go to Starbucks or buy the ten-dollar sugar-loaded smoothie every day. Try to buy your fruits and vegetables organic when you can.

Get Up and Go-Green Smoothie

2 cups of water or coconut water
1 handful of kale
1 handful of spinach
1 green apple or 1 kiwi
1 teaspoon of flaxseed or chia seeds or both
1 handful of almonds and a couple of walnuts

Wake Me Up (or pre-workout boost)

2 cups of almond milk, soy milk, or coconut milk
½ cup of black coffee
Half of a banana
1 tablespoon of almond butter or
peanut butter
Dash of cinnamon
Ice

Berry Delight Smoothie

2 cups of almond milk, soy milk, or coconut milk

1 handful of blueberries

1 handful of strawberries

Half of a banana

2 tablespoons of oatmeal

Flax seeds and or chia seeds or both

Ice

Mint Chip Smoothie

2 cups of vanilla almond milk

Half of a banana

1 handful of spinach

½ teaspoon of mint extract

Cacao nibs

Ice

Cleanse Smoothie

(great to keep your digestive system healthy)

2 cups of water

1 slice of pineapple

1 handful of spinach

¼ of celery stick

½ handful of parsley

1 quarter-size slice fresh ginger, peeled

Tips:

* For increasing your milk supply, add ½ teaspoon of brewer's yeast powder to any of the smoothies

* Adding nuts, seeds, or yogurt to these smoothies can help you feel fuller longer

* Add dates for sweetness. Only one or two. They are extremely high in natural sugar, but they are also high in fiber, iron, and potassium

* Add honey for sweetness and for a great natural energy boost

* Add organic protein powder, either vanilla or chocolate

for an energy boost and extra nutrients. I like the brand Orgain, available at Costco. Tera whey protein in vanilla or chocolate is also a good choice. It's organic and grass-fed

You Glow Girl

Usually I'll have a shake, with some sort of pure protein, then bananas, blueberries, frozen cherries, stevia, a vegetable mix of dynamic greens that goes in there, maca powder, and a little cacao. There's a collagen peptide that I've been loving—I've been seeing a difference! My nails are stronger and there's a healthier . . . how do you explain it? A glow. It's sort of that working from the inside-out thing.

—JENNIFER ANISTON, ON HER MORNING ROUTINE, THE
WELL+GOOD WEBSITE

Need I say more? If this is good for Jen, the queen of glow, then it's good for the rest of us simple mortals. Adding only chia seeds to your smoothie is so last season. There is a new magical powder to add to your smoothie so often that you can hardly keep up, but below is a list of some of the best. If you are breastfeeding, it is very important to check with your doctor first. In fact, I would start adding these ingredients to my smoothies once I stopped breastfeeding.

Collagen. Peptides are short-chain amino acids naturally derived from collagen protein. They are a key ingredient for glowing skin and a healthy body, as they ensure the cohesion, elasticity, and regeneration of skin, hair, tendons, cartilage, bones, and joints. Additionally, collagen supports digestion and satiety. Add one or two scoops to your fruit smoothies, coffee, or tea. It dissolves completely, and is tasteless and odorless. Recommended brands: TruMarine™ Collagen and Vital Proteins Collagen Peptides.

Bee pollen. According to the book *Bio Young*, bee pollen possesses the same range of estrogen effects as honey but in higher concentrations. In addition, bee pollen contains a good helping of protein. It can be eaten daily as a very potent food with wonderful anti-aging benefits. The author recommends a minimum of ten teaspoons of bee pollen a day to receive the full benefits. I add it to my smoothies and coffee. Try Sunfood Super Foods Raw Wild-Crafted Spanish Bee Pollen.

Maca. Increases collagen, stimulates hair growth, and makes hair thicker. It protects you against stress, increases your energy, improves memory, and acts as an antidepressant and antioxidant. What's more, maca protects the skin from sun damage, protects the liver, and strengthens your bones. The daily dose recommended is four teaspoons. To be honest, it gives a weird taste to my smoothies, so I only add half a teaspoon and don't consume it every day. Try Sunfood Raw Organic Maca Powder. **Please note: If you are breastfeeding, you should NOT consume maca.**

Cacao powder. Ancient Aztec and Mayan cultures considered cacao "food of the gods." Cacao adds a chocolatey flavor while adding a healthy antioxidant boost to your smoothies. With nutrients such as potassium, zinc, iron, and magnesium, cacao's benefits are endless, but buy it unsweetened. It can improve your memory, increase your bliss, reduce heart disease, boost immunity, and create loads of energy. In addition, cacao also helps to clear acne and can act as a protecting supplement for when you are exposed to the sun. Best of all, cacao can prevent premature aging as it belongs to the same group of antioxidants as green tea and red wine. The recommended dose is four teaspoons per day; do not exceed this recommendation. Try Sunfood Super Foods Organic Cacao Powder.

Go frozen

I really like the organic frozen smoothies ready to blend from Costco. These are great, especially for the first months as the last thing that you want to do is to cut vegetables and fruit. They have organic green and berry smoothies. Frozen vegetables and fruits are actually a great buy. They are cheaper and have almost the same nutrients as fresh produce. When I buy my veggies and fruits at the farmers market or organic super-markets, I wash and chop everything on the same day and then store them in small bags in the fridge already mixed for convenience.

Natural drinks

Warm water with lemon. There is no better way to start the day. Lemons are the most alkalizing food, which means they balance acids in your body and restore your pH level. They help boost your immune system, flush the digestive system, clean your liver, and they contain a high amount of vitamin C (great for anti-aging). According to research in Germany, there is evidence that drinking lemon water first thing in the morning can you help maintain a healthy weight. I have done this for the past fifteen years, along with other healthy habits, and I have always had a stable weight.

Ginger tea. Besides helping your body to absorb nutrients, it helps you feel full longer, acts as a fat burner, and helps to manage your glucose level. I add vanilla drops, apple or pear skin, and one cinnamon stick to my ginger tea. Vanilla is an antidepressant, is full of antioxidants, and helps to relax the muscles.

Green tea. Green tea is very effective at improving muscle synthesis and cutting the fat in your body. It also benefits your immune system by pro-tecting your body from free radical damage and toxins. On top of this, green tea is the best anti-aging drink there is, as it is full of antioxidants called polyphenols, which neutralize the effects of free radicals (molecules that damage healthy skin tissue). It also increases body-firming effects. I used to drink a lot of green tea before I had my baby, and I am sure this helped me with my skin and metabolism. During the summer, instead of asking for your iced latte with cream, swap it for iced green tea; it will help both your body and skin. According to scientific studies, the ideal amount to boost your metabolism is five cups per day. Go easy if you are breastfeeding or look for those with low caffeine.

Matcha tea. This type of tea has one of the highest concentrations of polyphenols. It boosts metabolism and can even protect the body from cancer and viruses. But do not go over two cups per day. In fact, I usually only have one.

Turmeric tea. It has digestive properties, is a natural antidepressant, and strengthens the immune system. Google Food Trends named turmeric the "breakout star" ingredient of 2016. Fresh turmeric root has been widely used thanks to its antioxidant, anti-inflammatory, and anticancer properties. Indians have used it for centuries. It also flushes toxins from the skin and helps eliminate acne.

Life Begins after Coffee

If you are breastfeeding, for the first few months, it's better for the body to not get used to coffee. I basically abstained from coffee for the first few months, just having a sip here and there. After months of sleepless nights, oh yes, I started to drink coffee every day. I even upgraded my coffeemaker.

Is There Such a Thing as Too Much Coffee?

The American Academy of Pediatrics recommends no more than three cups of coffee daily (200 to 300 milligrams of caffeine a day) for nursing women. While some of the caffeine mothers consume will end up in their breast milk, most research suggests that it is less than 1 percent. Some babies, particularly those under 6 months, have a harder time metabolizing caffeine than older infants. Infants who already have health problems might have more problems with mom's caffeine intake. Also, pay attention and if your baby is particularly irritable just after you had coffee and breastfed him, you may need to cut back or remove it altogether. Even if your baby is sensitive to the caffeine now, he may not be when he's a little older, so if you do have to stop or limit your caffeine intake, you can try again later.

Try sticking to only one cup per day to play it safe and, if you drink more than one, try a latte instead, which has less caffeine than regular brewed coffee. Don't forget to factor in other surprising sources of caffeine, including dark chocolate and certain pain relievers or cold remedies (you can usually check the label).

For your reference, one tall Starbucks coffee (12 oz.) has 375 milligrams of caffeine. One Starbucks Caffe Latte or Cappuccino, Grande (16 oz.) has 70 milligrams. I'm not even going to mention how much is in a Frappuccino, because the calories alone should keep your hands off! Save those for the occasional treat.

How to Make Your "Survival Juice" Healthier

Do not add any sugar or artificial sweeteners to your coffee. Artificial sweeteners trigger sugar receptors in the same way that real sugar does. It causes increased production of insulin and eventually, a sugar rush. However, cinnamon will help keep your sugar cravings at bay and prevent the accumulation of fat in the body by supporting the conversion of sugar into energy. It also speeds up your metabolism. If you have the habit of adding sugar or sweeteners to your coffee, start with half of your regular portion and after five days cut back until you end this habit.

Also, some lattes have anywhere from 200 to 290 calories. Just adding a small splash of milk to your Americano can save caffeine intake, a huge number of calories, and your pocketbook, too! A splash of milk or even substituting plant milk is also a great solution for bloating, as the bacteria in our colon can ferment lactose, leading to an excess production of gas. Milk can be a big trigger for those who are susceptible to bloating, which will occur only if your body has an issue with lactose. Otherwise, milk is a great source of calcium and protein. Just opt for skim or 2 percent.

According to *The Better Baby Book* by Drs. Lana Asprey and Dave Asprey, coffee is one of the most important things to buy organic as conventional coffees are sprayed heavily with pesticides, and variations in processing matter. Most of the coffee that I drink is from Colombia and is not organic. But don't stress about this when you are enjoying your well-deserved Starbucks Grande Latte (without whipped cream, I hope).

Did you know...

I know that the second thing (or perhaps the first) that you want to do after taking your baby from the bassinet or crib is drink your coffee but according to Dr. Steven Miller at the NeuroscienceDC blog, the best time to get your caffeine fix is 90 minutes after you wake up. This is because your level of cortisol, a hormone that increases alertness, naturally spikes right after you rise, so there's little additional benefit to drinking coffee then. But after an hour or two, production of the hormone starts to level off, and you can use the caffeine hit. Also, try to have your coffee in the morning, as caffeine takes eight to fourteen hours to leave your system and can negatively affect your sleep quality and, therefore, your productivity the next day. A 2013 study from Wayne State University and Henry Ford Hospital in Detroit concluded that when taken even six hours before bed, caffeine can decrease sleep by as much as one hour. I try to have only one coffee per day and I usually drink it mid-morning at home (to save some money). Sometimes I don't drink it all or, as many moms do, reheat it several times throughout the morning just to end up drinking an "accidental" iced coffee. If I know that I will meet someone for coffee later, I skip my morning coffee.

I prefer mine with almond or soy milk and add cinnamon instead of sugar.

Mommy Cocktail

This is the favorite "cocktail" drink for pregnant or breastfeeding friends:

Mix ½ cup of sparkling water and ½ cup flavored water (lemon or berries). Crush some berries and put them at the bottom of a cocktail glass. Add the water and then top with mint leaves. Enjoy!

Healthy Eating

Even though I have no formal education as a nutritionist, I've always been passionate about learning about and improving my healthy-eating habits. I've also been lucky to have found and worked with knowledgeable professionals who have helped me be a better mom while maintaining a nutritionally balanced diet.

Here are few simple tips that I've learned and wanted to share with you. This chapter has been reviewed by Heidi Parish, a nutritionist based in San Diego, California for safety and accuracy, but it's always a good idea to consult with your doctor before changing your eating habits, especially if you are breastfeeding.

Menu
Upon Waking

Start with one cup of warm water with lemon first thing in the morning.

Breakfast

The most important meal of the day. Research shows that people who have breakfast are up to 50 percent less likely to become obese; a nutritious breakfast eliminates the need to snack and to have oversized meals later in the day. As busy moms it is difficult to squeeze in, but this is essential. Try to eat within the first half hour of waking. It will help keep your energy up throughout the day.

Hot chocolate with cinnamon (remember my mom's advice), green smoothie or berry smoothie, whole wheat toast with almond butter or a bit of strawberry jam, one egg (sometimes with bacon or avocado or both), or oatmeal with blueberries, flaxseed, chia seeds, and a drizzle of honey. Did I mention that my appetite during the first few months was huge?

Snack
Fruit salad with Greek yogurt, almonds, honey, and chia seeds.

Lunch
Lentils with chicken (lentils are high in iron and a great choice after delivery) or chicken with brown rice and salad or butternut squash soup with half of a cheese sandwich and veggies are great options.

Snack
Acai bowl or banana with almond butter.

Dinner
Steak with sweet potatoes (which offer more nutritional value than a white potato) and a spinach or chicken salad with avocado or salmon, a bit of brown rice and asparagus, and then chocolate mousse or some dark chocolate almonds.

You need a lot of iron to recover from labor (beans, lentils, dark green leafy vegetables, whole grains, and meat), plenty of fresh vegetables and fruit, especially those high in vitamin C such as oranges (and their juice), kiwis, red peppers, and strawberries, as they will help your body to absorb iron.

Your Key Ingredients
A balanced diet contains protein for growth and repair, fruit and vegetables for micronutrients for nerve and cellular health, whole-grain carbohydrates for energy and fiber, dairy for calcium, and healthy fats for heart, hormone and brain health.

Protein
Eggs
For decades eggs were slandered as unhealthy because they are high in cholesterol but, in fact, eggs contain a great balance of healthy fat and protein, so eating them helps you to feel both energized and satisfied. Most of the nutrients in the egg are in the yolk, along with half of the protein and all of the healthy fat. So eating just egg whites is not recommended. I eat an egg every single day, sunny side up. They are rich in iron and biotin, which help keep your skin and hair full and healthy. Do not forget to wash your eggs before cracking them. And finally, look for the term "pasture-raised eggs." I used to buy cage-free eggs thinking it was the healthiest option and the best for the chickens and the environment. It turns out that, while cage-free means that the chickens were not in cages, they can still be confined in very close quarters inside a building where they are standing in their own muck and can barely move. They have little or no access to the outdoors and consume a corn or soy diet. *Free range* and *vegetarian raised* can mean the same thing. Just buy pasture-raised eggs, which means the chickens were raised in the outdoors . . . in the pasture, how it's supposed to be!

Fish
Fish contains a lot of omega-3 fatty acids, which does wonders for your skin and body. Interestingly, studies have found that people who consume omega-3s regularly are less likely to be depressed. This is because omega-3s produce antioxidants and detoxification enzymes that work against high levels of stress. My favorite fish is salmon, one of the most omega-3-rich foods you can eat. Try to eat fish at least once a week.

The Seafood Watch Program can help you choose which fish is best for you and the environment (i.e., sustainable and with a lower mercury content). There are a lot of questions regarding which type of fish to eat, such as wild or farm-raised. Recommended choices are wild salmon from Alaska, where fisheries are extremely well-managed (and the fish may have fewer antibiotics, pollutants, and saturated fat, and more calcium, iron, and zinc than farmed fish), black cod, albacore tuna, rainbow trout, and arctic char. For more information, visit: www.seafoodwatch.org

Grass-Fed Steak

According to *Time* magazine's *Special Edition 2017: 100 Healthiest Foods to Satisfy Your Hunger*, grilled steak is one of the tastiest ways to load up on iron and protein. Red meat tends to get a lot of negative press, but grass-fed varieties can be part of a healthy diet and keep you full. Consume in moderation (I eat it once a week) and try not to burn it, as charred steak can produce chemicals that are considered carcinogens by major health groups. It is very important that you buy steaks that are both organic and grass-fed. If you can only choose one, choose grass-fed over organic.

Oils and Nuts
Almonds

Almonds are high in fiber, which means that they take a while to digest and, therefore, suppress hunger for a longer period of time. (Something we need as busy moms!) Raw almond butter is a great way to include almonds in your daily menu. Almonds also help the body produce more milk. Another great choice is walnuts, the king of omega-3 fatty acid content. I don't like the taste of walnuts (don't they taste like soap?), so I add a couple to my smoothies every day and eat them blended. You don't need to eat too many to receive all the benefits.

Olive oil

Olive oil contributes to improved cardiovascular health and optimizes cholesterol levels. It contains antioxidants and brain-boosting plant chemicals. Look for the term "cold-pressed," which means the oil is extracted using only pressure rather than chemicals, and choose extra virgin olive oil.

Vegetables and Fruits
Apples

Eating an apple a day may, in fact, help keep the doctor away. A study mentioned in *Time Special Edition: 100 Healthiest Foods to Satisfy Your Hunger* found that regular apple eaters used fewer prescription medications than those who eat them less often, perhaps due to the naturally present antioxidants and gut-healthy fiber. Plus, apples contain pectin, a compound that slows digestion and promotes fullness.

Avocado

Avocados have a high content of healthy fat and they are loaded with fiber, so you stay full longer. Another plus? They are high in potassium. Low levels of potassium can lead to greater risk of mood disturbances, irritability, depression, and tension.

Berries

They contain a lot of antioxidants and contribute to collagen production, which may prevent some age-related skin damage. The darker the berry, the higher content of vitamins C and E. Just have a handful of blueberries every day.

Broccoli

High in antioxidants and fiber, and low in calories.

Kale

It is a superfood rich in antioxidants. It is also high in fiber, which helps with the digestive process.

Kiwis

Kiwis may be small, but they contain twice as much vitamin C as oranges (just one has all the vitamin C that you need for a day), more fiber than apples, and as much vitamin E as an avocado. All this for fewer than 50 calories.

Grains and Seeds
Chia seeds

These are loaded with nutrients: fiber, protein, omega-3 fatty acids, and vitamin B1, which is called the anti-stress vitamin.

Flaxseeds

They are a great source of magnesium, which can help increase energy. They also help with digestion and reduce sugar cravings. If you add two tablespoons of flax seeds to your smoothie or oatmeal daily, you will have healthier skin, hair, and nails.

Lentils

Lentils, as well as other beans, such as black beans and chickpeas (which, by the way, are considered an anti-aging powerhouse), offer iron, protein and fiber, which help make you feel full longer. It is one of the most filling foods available.

Oatmeal

Oats are a fiber-rich food, making them an excellent weight loss option because they help you feel full longer. They also help with milk production. Always go for old-fashioned oats or quick oats rather than packaged instant oatmeal, which has added salt and sugar.

Quinoa

Quinoa is one of the world's most popular health foods and there are so many reasons why: It is high in protein, fiber, minerals (especially magnesium, potassium, zinc, and iron), and antioxidants. It contains all the essential amino acids that we need for good health.

Truth about whole grains

Carbohydrates are an important source of energy. They have been given a bad reputation by fad diets that eliminate all carbs for weight loss, but they are an important part of our diet for energy and cellular health.

Whole grains have more fiber than refined grains, so they are a better option, but they won't help you lose weight. Whole-grain cereals, bread, and pastas have about the same number of calories as their more-processed counterparts and are very easy to binge on. But whole grains are an important source of energy in your diet and have greater nutritional value than refined choices. The reason that carbohydrates and whole grains are often a spot of contention in diets is due to portion size. The usual recommendation is a small amount of carbohydrates accompanied with lean protein as a valid nutrition choice for meals and snacks. However, the portion sizes we have in America are ridiculous; thus many people gain weight from eating too many calories, not necessarily carbohydrates.

Dairy
Kefir

I only found out about kefir recently. so I was late to the party! Kefir is a fermented milk product (cow, goat, or sheep milk) that tastes like a drinkable yogurt. It is considered healthier than yogurt, as it contains live enzymes and more strains of beneficial bacteria. It boosts immunity, supports detoxification, heals various digestive problems, and helps with allergies and asthma. It is generally tolerated by people who are lactose intolerant (kefir is fermented and relatively low in lactose). I buy the low-fat, unsweetened version, and usually have it with some blueberries, granola, and honey.

Yogurt

It's important to have adequate calcium intake for bone health, and yogurt is a great source. I choose Greek yogurt, which offers more protein than regular yogurt. Buy unsweetened and sweeten it on your own with fresh fruit, honey, or agave.

Buy Organic When Possible

Keep this in mind when you are feeding your baby. Based on the results of ongoing pesticide tests performed on produce and collected by federal agencies, pesticides and chemicals can have adverse effects on health, especially during fetal development and childhood. Buy organic whenever possible.

The Environmental Working Group's Shopper's Guide to Pesticides identifies fruits and vegetables that have the highest and lowest pesticide residues.

The Shopper's Guide to Pesticides in Produce.

The Clean 15
Beginning with the cleanest: avocados, sweet corn, pineapples, cabbage, onions, sweet peas, papaya, asparagus, mangos, eggplant, honeydew, kiwis, cantaloupe, cauliflower and broccoli.

Dirty Dozen
The 12 most-contaminated and sprayed fruits and veggies beginning with the dirtiest are: strawberries, spinach, nectarines, apples, grapes, peaches, cherries, pears, tomatoes, celery, potatoes and sweet bell peppers.

For more information, visit The Environmental Working Group's website at www.ewg.org. This is a nonprofit, non-partisan organization that works to empower people to get to know their environment and protect their health. Their website can tell you not only what pesticides are on your food, but also what's in your tap water and shampoo, what's lurking in the cleaners underneath your sink, how to avoid health-harming chemicals at home, and more. You just need to enter your ZIP code.

———————————

Month 3

Three months is a big milestone for the baby. At that age, they start to show their personalities. They smile, are more alert, and interact more with the world around them. It is a big milestone for you, too. It is time to work on you! You've had your two months' leave, you've focused on the baby, and you have more confidence in your skills as a mom. Hopefully, over these two months you have lost a bit of weight. At least the baby, the placenta, and fluids are gone from your body!

Healthy Eating

I remember when I was pregnant, breakfast was very important for me. Every day I had oatmeal with banana; a spinach, kiwi, and kale smoothie; and egg with toast. After the baby, the only thing that changed is that I added a cup of hot chocolate! At my third month, I realized that I was still eating the same as I had when I was pregnant. I was breastfeeding, but I did not need to consume that many extra calories, even if they were healthy ones. Don't have a big breakfast just for the sake of it. If you are really hungry, have it.

To lose weight initially, focus on your nutrition rather than on increasing your physical activity. A study from the University of Missouri found that participants who attended Weight Watchers meetings for twelve weeks lost about nine pounds; those who just joined a gym shed about three pounds. For most people trying to lose weight, eating small, frequent meals and snacks usually leads to better results, as this usually helps keep you more satisfied throughout the day and may lead to better choices. Exercise is still healthy for you, don't get me wrong, but it can burn only a small portion of the calories consumed during the day. If you eat more calories than you burn, then you will gain weight. Conversely, if you consume fewer calories than your body burns then you will lose weight. Cutting 500 calories a day will lead to a one-pound weight loss at the end of the week. Rebooting diet and exercise simultaneously may not be a good idea. It may be easier to make one change at a time. The positive results you see may then be a motivator to go for the next change.

Menu

Sorry! We need to start cutting the calories a bit.

Breakfast

A cup of hot water with lemon upon waking and water and green tea throughout the day.

Oatmeal with fruit or one egg with whole wheat toast and avocado, or an oatmeal smoothie with almond butter.

Lunch

Chicken salad, turkey wrap, or veggie burger (no bread or just one slice). Add a salad or brown rice with chickpeas, kale, tomatoes, cucumber, and a bit of lemon juice.

Dinner

Steak, salmon, or chicken, with a salad or stir-fried vegetables (use coconut oil) with quinoa.

When you are cooking dinner, plan ahead by making extra to have on hand for the week. You can prepare tuna salad (use lime juice and veggies, and, instead of mayo, add avocado) and keep it in the fridge.

I am not a big fan of salads. They don't fill me up! When I was stuck with my weight, I tried to have chicken salad for dinner every day. (I know, so boring.) I added a couple of croutons, a bit of Parmesan cheese, oranges, and a homemade dressing (olive oil, balsamic vinegar, salt, and pepper) to make it more fun. I also liked some quinoa in my salad at night for protein and carbs. I find that a dinner salad with quinoa will satisfy my hunger for a longer period than a salad without any whole grain. Toasted nuts, dried fruits (small amounts), and avocados are great additions. This light meal really helped me to shed the extra pounds more quickly.

Snack Ideas

Snacks are often where people go wrong when it comes to eating good food on the go. Good snacks would be something like baked kale chips, apple or bananas with peanut or almond butter and cinnamon, plain Greek yogurt with fresh fruit, green or berry smoothie, or a whey protein shake. Also, fruits such as watermelon, strawberries, and grapefruit, which are about 90 percent water, are great as a snack. Other suggestions are veggies with hummus or tahini, chia seed pudding (see recipe forthcoming), acai bowls (see recipe forthcoming), smoked salmon on whole wheat crackers, or Jessica Alba's favorite snack—popcorn. (I enjoyed this one very much until I put the popcorn in the microwave longer than required and the bag started to burn. Then I tried to do it in the traditional way, and I burned the pan. My husband has banned me from making this snack.) Skinnypop brand offers single-serving bags that are 100 calories so there is no need to worry about serving size or a large bag of popcorn going stale. Tons of snack-sized, pre-portioned snacks are available at grocery stores (nuts, trail mix, turkey jerky, hummus with whole grain pita, pretzels with almond butter). It's great to have these on hand for a quick snack and have them in the car and diaper bag as a healthy choice on the go. The more satisfied you feel, the less tempted you will be to snack on empty calories or binge later.

Here are some recipes that are quick and easy to make. Some of them have ingredients that you can share with your baby when he starts solids:

Acai Bowl

1 pouch frozen acai   1 banana
¼ cup of almond, soy, or skim milk   Bunch of blueberries

Blend all the ingredients for 30 seconds. You want a thicker ice cream consistency for bowls, or a thinner liquid consistency for smoothies. Serve with granola on top.

Chia Seed Pudding

1 banana   ½ teaspoon of lemon juice
Half a can of unsweetened coconut   1 small pinch of salt
   milk (reduced fat)   5 tablespoons of chia seeds
1 teaspoon of vanilla extract   1 teaspoon of sugar or honey

Combine all the ingredients except the chia seeds in a blender for one minute. Add the chia seeds and let sit for at least 10 minutes, then blend for 30 sec. Place it in a sealed container and put it in the fridge for a couple of hours to set. Add banana or blueberries or enjoy as is!

For an easier recipe with less mess, just soak the chia seeds overnight in almond milk and add a few drops of vanilla extract. Add fruit and nuts for extra energy.

Banana and Chocolate Overnight Oats

1 cup almond milk   ½ tablespoon cacao powder
2 scoops protein powder (chocolate   4 tablespoons rolled oats
   or vanilla)   ½ tablespoon chia seeds (optional)
½ ripe banana, sliced

Using a container with a lid, place all the ingredients in a container and stir. Close the lid and shake to mix well. Place in the refrigerator for at least eight hours, or overnight. In the morning, just grab a spoon and enjoy.

Banana Pancakes

½ cup of oat flour

1 tablespoon of cacao powder (optional)

1 tablespoon of coconut sugar (optional, if the banana doesn't make it sweet enough)

½ teaspoon of baking powder

⅓ cup of almond milk or regular milk (add a bit more if you need it)

1 mashed banana

1 egg (or add a little more milk, instead)

1 teaspoon of vanilla extract

Mix all the ingredients in a blender and then let sit for 5 minutes. Put your pan on a medium heat. Add small portions of the batter to the pan so that you have room for at least 4–5 pancakes.

This is a great option for breakfast for you and your baby (from 7 or 8 months). Keep the leftovers in the fridge (I pack them individually in Ziploc bags) and just put them in the toaster when you are craving something sweet. I add almond butter and a bit of honey to mine.

Quinoa Oatmeal

This recipe is the daily breakfast of a dear friend of mine. She cooks it on Sunday night and then enjoys this high-protein breakfast every day during the week. This is great as a breakfast or just to have in the middle of the afternoon instead of a high-calorie snack. Reheat it in the microwave for one minute.

1 cup of quinoa

1 cup of water

2 cups of soy or almond milk

½ cup of raisins

Dash of cinnamon

Rinse the quinoa and pour it in a pot. Add enough water (about one cup).

Bring it to boil, then add two cups of soy/almond milk. Let it simmer, stirring with a wooden spoon occasionally. Add more soy milk ground cinnamon and raisins. Continue to simmer until the grain is soft and the milk is almost absorbed. Enjoy with flax and chia seeds and blueberries. Refrigerate in a glass container.

Roasted Chickpeas

This is the favorite snack of another close friend of mine, who prefers salty snacks. I am not a big fan of chickpeas, but I must say that when you roast them, they taste delicious and help keep you full throughout the day.

1 can of chickpeas   1 pinch of salt
1 tablespoon of olive oil   1 pinch of oregano

Heat the oven to 400F. Rinse the chickpeas and dry as much as possible with paper towels. If you can, let them air dry for a few minutes. Place the chickpeas on a baking sheet. Coat with olive oil and sprinkle with salt and then stir with a spatula to mix evenly. Roast for 30 minutes. Take them out of the oven and toss with oregano.

To receive more delicious and simple recipes in your inbox, sign up at saragaviria.com.

Exercise

Once you have taken off the first several pounds, exercise is very important, both to keep your body healthy and to keep your mind strong. According to the American Psychological Association, exercise relieves stress and reduces depression.

After you get the OK from the doctor, I recommend a minimum of three workout sessions per week, plus 30 minutes of walking every day. You don't need to leave the house to work out. There are so many Instagram accounts or DVDs with exercise routines. I did Alexa Jean Fitness (check her Instagram account) and a Tracy Anderson post-pregnancy workout video (Amazon). I did the 30-day ab challenge from Alexa Jean Fitness, which you can download on your phone and do at home with no equipment. You only have to do it five times a week and it takes less than 30 minutes. I did it for 30 days and even though I skipped some days, I still saw a difference.

When you start to feel stronger and ready to do some exercises on your own, try to incorporate some plank variations into your routine. They are not only the best way to get your abs back, but you'll also see an overall transformation in your body, as they engage more than 20 muscles, including shoulders, legs, glutes, and arms. Planks can be challenging at first, but they're one of the most effective and safest ways to exercise your body. Start with the beginner exercises and practice holding each move for 30 seconds. My personal favorites are the traditional standard plank or high plank, side planks, and plank with shoulder touches.

At the end of month three, try to incorporate exercise or any kind of physical activity into your routine. Go to the gym, go for a walk with the stroller, do some yoga poses, or dance in front of your baby (they love that). You can do simple exercises such as squats, lunges, and abs, which work a lot of muscle groups effectively. Start with three sets of 10 and work up to four sets of 15. It is very important when you start to exercise that you start easy, and then build up. You know your body better than anyone else. Be aware of your limits and when it is better not to push yourself.

Make sure that you are always on the move. Remember, it will be good not only for your body but for your mind, too. Plan your day ahead. If you are meeting a friend for coffee in the afternoon, try to have some exercise in the morning while your baby naps. If you want to watch a TV program at night, plan to do some squats or ab exercises while you watch. You can always find 10 to 15 minutes to move your skeleton.

Try to have a healthy attitude toward exercise. Don't torture yourself if you are not able to do it every day. Having said that, you DO need to be consistent if you want to see changes. Once you have achieved your weight goal, you can slow down a bit. But remember, if you want to have a nice figure, exercise is a habit, a lifestyle.

At the end of this month, you may want to start weighing yourself every day. I know some doctors, trainers, and weight loss experts tell you not to weigh yourself every day, but for me it really worked. It was the only way to measure my success. This is also supported by several studies. A 2015 study at Cornell University found that daily weigh-ins helped people lose more weight, keep it off, and maintain that loss, even after two years. Also, at the 2015 American Heart Association conference, researchers said that monitoring weight allows people to see what effect their diet is having. Participants who weigh themselves daily also avoided overeating. Those people reported feeling confident about avoiding temptation, the study found. That's because they were more aware of overeating.

Make sure you write down your weight. It makes sense. "When we encounter new information and want to learn from it, we should force ourselves to do something with the data. It is not enough for your bathroom scale to send daily updates to an app on your phone. If you want to lose the weight, force yourself to plot those measurements on graph paper and you will be more likely to choose a salad over a hamburger at lunch," according to *Smarter Faster Better, The Secrets of Productive in Life and Business* by Charles Duhigg. After I got to my goal, I did not weigh myself every day. Who has time with a baby crawling around the house, right? I do weigh myself a couple of times a month, and also when I come back from a vacation or feel that I have not exercised and or eaten properly for a couple of weeks.

Continue with three main meals and two healthy snacks per day, exercising three times a week, walking for at least 30 minutes every day, and doing the ab challenge or at least a good set of planks during months 4 and 5. It will get easier, week after week.

Month 6

You are finally feeling like your old self again and are amazed by the things your baby can do every day. My baby started crawling in his sixth month and then things got a bit complicated. It is when I started to understand what people meant when they said, "I don't exercise. I just run after the baby all day." I always thought that was nonsense but now, I completely understand!

Your diet may suffer, too. Between the cooking, cleaning up, and making sure that the baby stays alive every minute (if you have an early crawler), you barely have time to eat.

I have never been the best cook, and I was not interested at all in the subject. To say that I was overwhelmed when I started cooking for my baby is an understatement. I even had to watch how to cut a zucchini on YouTube. (Do you know you're supposed to leave the skin on?) I am also very messy: one apple puree and the kitchen looked like Thanksgiving dinner disaster!

Healthy Eating

Menu
Upon Waking
Drink hot water with lemon, and water and green tea throughout the day

Breakfast
Smoothie with oatmeal or egg and wheat toast

Lunch (on the go, the baby is so active!)

* You can eat the soup or vegetable puree you make for your baby—just add salt, pepper, and shredded cheese and have a piece of toast with half an avocado

* Open-face sandwich with organic lunch meat (watch preservatives and sodium content) or leftover grilled meats from the previous night's dinner. You can also use thinly sliced leftover chicken breast. (Maybe make extra just for lunches.). Swiss cheese is a good option (lower in calories and fat than cheddar). I like thin-sliced cheeses because they reduce the calories but still cover the whole sandwich. You could also spread a little goat cheese on the bread. A little goes a long way.

* Brown rice sushi from the deli

* Whole wheat bagel with smoked salmon and low-fat cream cheese on one side only

* Organic veggie burger (find them in the freezer section) with one slice of whole-wheat bread, a bit of mustard, and a salad

* Tuna with cherry tomatoes, peppers, and lemon. I put some garlic in a heated pan, then I add tomatoes and peppers. After three minutes, I add a can of tuna, mix everything, and add lemon and some organic ketchup (my taste!).

Snacks

Fruit or almonds on the go (keep in your diaper bag or car), edamame, protein bar (I'm enjoying the GoMacro and Kind Bars, right now). Remember, a good calorie target for a snack is about 150 to 250 calories, depending on your weight goals and caloric needs. And in general, a good recommendation for sugar content is no more than 3 grams of sugar per 100 calories. Of course, some sugar is natural, so this needs to be taken into account. Have it only in the morning.

Dinner

Steak or shrimp quesadilla with veggies, whole wheat pasta with chicken or tuna in tomato sauce and peppers, or salmon with brown rice and some veggies. The world! I am so hungry and happy that I can eat!

If you are in a rush or too lazy/tired to cook at night, have an egg and brown rice. Put half of an avocado on top and a dash of olive oil.

Dessert (occasionally)

Chocolate mousse, Mochi chocolate ice cream, granola cereal with almond milk, or Greek yogurt with honey and cinnamon.

Don't forget your vitamins!

If you are still breastfeeding, I assume that you are taking your prenatal vitamins. If you have stopped breastfeeding, you can continue taking your prenatal vitamins or switch to a multivitamin. You may not be consuming enough of certain vitamins and minerals that are vital to your health and energy level. It's always best to get these nutrients by eating a well-rounded diet. That said, you're a beyond-busy mom and the incessant daily demands of looking after your baby means you probably don't eat as well as you should. Taking a multivitamin can help fill in those nutritional gaps. Plus, it can help give you radiant skin, hair and nails. I like Garden Of Life or Mykind Organic Women's Once Daily Multivitamin, which are made from real food (over 30 organic fruits, vegetables and herbs). Talk with your doctor to find the best multivitamin for you.

You Can Keep Some Sweets

You already know that sugar is bad for you, right? Scientists have recently published numerous studies showing that fat might not be so bad after all. But sugar definitely is. It makes you overweight and can also give you wrinkles! (It breaks down collagen, the substance that makes your skin look plump, youthful, and lifted.) If you have a sweet tooth like me, satisfy it with dark chocolate. Dark chocolate in moderation is actually good for you. (I was so happy when I found out about this several years ago). It turns out that it has a wide variety of powerful antioxidants and healthy fats. Look for chocolate with at least 80 percent cocoa for maximum anti-oxidants and less added sugar. (Lindt, Green and Black, Ghirardelli, and usually Swiss and other European chocolates have that percentage). If you deprive yourself completely of your guilty pleasure, you begin to obsess and find yourself diving into a big chocolate cake at some point. For home baking, use healthy sweeteners like xylitol (from hardwood, not corn) or stevia. For the most delicious and simple recipe for sugar-free chocolate cake (ready in 20 minutes!), sign up at saragaviria.com to receive it in your inbox.

Exercise

I lost the last of my baby weight at six months. It was a slow but consistent process. My baby was very active, and it took a lot of energy to keep up with him, so I was able to cut back my exercise routine. I didn't worry too much because I was still doing my daily walks; I just focused on eating very healthy and tried to sleep when I could. When I felt up to it, I did some yoga stretch poses or abs, or I would go to a class once in a while. I felt that there was no need to do weights for my arms—carrying my baby and his car seat around was enough.

Abs? What about Your butt?

My sister. Remember my lovely sister? She came for Christmas when my son was eight months old, after not having seen me for five months. She looked at me from every angle and said in a very serious tone: "I need to tell you something."

    Me: "What is that?"
    Sister: "You have no butt."

I was so focused on getting a flat stomach that I completely forgot about my butt. As you lose your baby weight and extra fat, this perky part of your anatomy (was mine perky? I don't remember!) will suffer. As if we didn't have enough body issues!

But why does this happen? I learned from Kim Vopni, known as The Fitness Doula, that during pregnancy our center of gravity shifts and affects our posture, so our body tries to overcompensate in other areas to acclimate this change in dynamic, as well as the extra weight. Women tend to counterbalance this shift by pushing their hips forward and tightening up their lower back into the tailbone pulling their butt inward. After overcompensating in this way for nine months, this new frame becomes normal, thus making the butt being pulled inward appear flatter. This is why butt-lifting jeans are so popular!

Just remember to add squats and lunges to your workout. I personally like to include squat and lunge variations to my routine because they help keep my muscles active and engaged, especially on the days where I have very little time to work out. If you are feeling strong enough, add weights. Just keep in mind that the more time you dedicate to exercise, the better results you'll see. Personally, I really like Alexa Jean Fitness and follow her on Instagram. She shares great exercises and routines. Or even better, buy her 30-day leg and butt challenge. She usually offers them at special rates or as a combo: abs, and legs and butt. Also, I like the Brooke Burke Body app; she has very effective "booty workouts."

Try to commit to a healthy lifestyle. Your body reacts to how you feed it mentally, spiritually, and physically. Don't beat yourself up when you can't do it every day, but try to incorporate it into your daily routine. It is never too late and it is an amazing feeling.

Sleep Training and Multitasking

According to baby books, by month six (some say by month four, but I don't know where those babies are from), your baby should sleep through the night. If you are ready (or forced by your husband, as I was) to start sleep training, you can multitask while you sleep-train your baby. I know, it's going to break your heart, but you might as well burn some calories while you're at it. If you're holding him to help him get relaxed and ready for sleep, you can do some squats. If that is too difficult for you or you just don't have the balance, try to move side to side with your knees slightly bent; this will work your inner thighs. Or just stand still and move your leg backwards; this will work your lower butt.

Once you put him in the crib, you could do squats and leg extensions. If you are leaving his room and entering every three to five minutes, put a mattress outside the room and do 20 reps of different ab exercises and 40- to 60-second planks, front and then side-by-side (as seen here). Time will fly by more quickly.

If you are reading this and thinking, "Give me a freaking break! I am not going to exercise while I am trying to get my crying baby to sleep," what about a foot or hand massage (yours!) while your baby is in the crib and you are next to him? You can use his body lotion or diaper cream: Try Aquaphor, AD, or The Honest Company Healing Balm. All of these have great moisturizing ingredients.

Month 7–10

Healthy Eating

It's important to have a good breakfast, and remember—small, frequent meals are ideal for sustained energy. Now that you are more adjusted to your new life as a mom, be conscious of the size of your portions and adjust appropriately. The following is a way to eyeball your serving size:

Menu

* Protein: size of the palm of your hand
* Starchy carbs (rice, pasta, or potatoes): size of your fist
* Whole grains: size of two fists
* Fruits and vegetables: size of two palms
* Healthy fats (olive oil, peanut or almond butter): size of two thumbs

This works for a salad but also for stir-fry or the basic dinner of chicken grilled with roasted vegetables and brown rice. With salads, it is important to not overdo the dressing. Always ask for it on the side. I really like just using olive oil and vinegar (especially when out) so you can control the amount of calories being added on top. Fresh lemon juice with a little olive oil and herbs or mustard is a great versatile dressing for salads or to top roasted or steamed veggies. From this month on, try not to have fruit as a snack.

Here's a tip I learned: Make your plate a rainbow. I remember asking my pediatrician about how to ensure that my son was getting all the vitamins and nutrients he needs, and the doctor said, "Make sure that he eats a variety of vegetables and fruits of many colors." This is definitely something that we can apply to ourselves, too. It is so obvious, but we still forget. The more brightly colored your plate is, the broader the range of nutrients.

Do not diet; you are creating a lifestyle. Be mindful of your snacks. Are you always snacking on sweets? Make sure to have something nutritious and filling and, of course, easy to make. You are also starting to cook for your baby (hopefully healthy and organic when you can), so just cook bigger portions and have their purees as a snack. Drink lots of water and green tea. If you like sweets, just have one sweet per day. Don't worry and don't give up; it requires time. Our bodies need time to change and react and it might be slower for some people and faster for others.

The Skinny on Being Too Thin

Being too skinny probably doesn't sound like a problem, but it can be for some. And it happened to me. As I mentioned before, my baby started crawling a bit early and it took me a long time to prepare food for him. The house was getting messier and I spent the whole day cooking, driving my baby to classes, breastfeeding, walking with the stroller, and putting stuff away at home. I was so busy that my eating started to suffer. I was underweight by four pounds and when you are already thin, four pounds can look like eight. My parents and friends became concerned and said that I was too skinny. But working hard to lose the pregnancy weight for six months, I took it graciously as a compliment. Then one day I went to a dance class at my gym, as I enjoy it very much and consider myself a decent dancer. I was in the first row and as I started dancing, I looked at myself in the mirror. I was wearing leggings and a tight top and it was the first time in months that I had looked at myself in a big mirror for more than 30 seconds. That's when noticed. I thought, "Oh my god, I am too skinny, too pale. My skin is dry and dull." The dance routine was sexy, but I did not feel sexy at all, not even feminine. The next day, I called . . . who else? My sister.

Me: "I went to my dancing class yesterday, and I just realized that I am too skinny."

Sister: "Yes, you are. I already told you. You don't even have a butt anymore."

Me: "I did not even feel good at the class. I look terrible. What I am going to do?"

Sister: (after a long pause) "EAT!" (I think she was rolling her eyes.)

As usual, she was right. I was not paying attention to my eating. I was skipping lunch, and I was so tired at night that I just ate whatever was quick to make, such as three bowls of quinoa cereal with almond milk. I had to make a conscious effort to eat more, while still eating healthily.

If this is your problem, make calories count by adding healthy fats to all meals and eating more nutrient-dense choices. Nut butters are nutrient-dense and a great addition to increase calories. I started adding more protein to my breakfast. One full egg and one egg white, almond butter or avocado in my smoothie, protein bars and nuts for snacks, and whole wheat or quinoa pasta with veggies at night. I made sure that I had protein at lunch and dinner. Adding more snacks, especially one before bed, is also helpful. Often, drinking calories is an easier way to add them to your diet. Calories that you drink are often not as filling as those you eat, so you can have a smoothie between meals and still be hungry for your main meal. Once again, the goal is to be more conscious of what you are eating. Sometimes the appetite will spark if you eat smaller meals. When the body is "starving," hunger goes to the wayside.

I also focused more on my stretch workouts and gentle yoga than cardio and weights. I did not gain the weight straight away though because I was still breastfeeding, but I had more energy and felt stronger, and my skin looked nicer.

Exercise

At this point, you might not have reached your pre-pregnancy weight goal. In that case, continue with the sixth month plan and make sure to include cardio and resistance training (both are important) in your workout routines. For cardio, it does not have to be running. What about a spinning class, a fast-paced walk with your baby in the stroller, or a Zumba class after you put your baby to bed? I know it sounds exhausting, but once you are dancing and sweating, you will be happy you did it. As I heard from someone once, no one regrets working out after they did it!

Here's an interval session you can try: 30 seconds of exercise (anything that takes you out of your comfort zone—jumping, running, or walking fast) followed by 10 seconds rest. Do this eight times, then rest for 60 seconds and repeat up to eight times. With intervals, you not only burn calories for the session, but will carry on burning calories for hours afterward and increase aerobic capacity. Only do this type of training twice a week and on non-consecutive days. Also, do not forget about resistance work. This type of workout is actually more beneficial for losing weight than cardio alone. Remember, the more muscle you have, the more fat you burn! More about this later in Month 11–12.

I also recommend the Stroller Strides program. If you can afford the membership, you can go every day. Now that your baby is a bit older, (7–12 months) he will start to enjoy the class, too. You will be able to stay after the class and make mommy friends as well. More about this in the chapter *How to Make Friends*.

Month 11–12

Your baby's routine is getting more predictable and he is napping for longer periods of time (thank God!). You have mastered the art of cooking for your baby, you feel stronger, and you are sleeping seven to eight hours straight (hopefully!). You have achieved your weight goal (or are almost there!), you don't feel awkward in your mommy classes anymore, and you have actually made a couple of mommy friends.

Healthy Eating

What to Eat After Your Workout

You finally find the time to go to the gym or exercise at home and after you finish, you go back immediately to your mommy duties. This is a very common mistake. Please, find the time to eat within 15 to 45 minutes after you work out. According to the Journal of the International Society of Sports Medicine, your body will automatically use the calories for repair and recovery. Consuming some protein and carbohydrates is best immediately after exercise. This prevents dips in energy later on and controls insatiable appetite.

Experts recommend a liquid meal that contains protein and carbohydrates. These drinks don't require a lot of digestion; therefore the nutrients get into your system fast, allowing your body to jump-start the recovery process.

A good example is a protein shake made with half a banana (or without to make it less complicated), one or two scoops of protein or whey powder, and almond milk, coconut water, or water. This is perfect for us moms on the go!

Be Mindful

Pay special attention to your hunger and fullness cues, to what your body needs and what it does not. This means eating mindfully. This can be difficult to do as a mom balancing the needs of her family, but try to focus on eating as a singular activity, (I know, very hard. Just try when you can).

As your baby is eating a greater variety of food, don't get in the habit of "a bite for him and a bite for me" or finishing the goodies left on your child's plate (such as the leftover crusts from a grilled cheese sandwich). The calories will add up quickly! Eat lots of berries; they are great for your skin. Keep protein bars and almonds in your car or in your diaper bag to keep up your energy levels. Drink lots of water and green tea.

Exercise

You have been enjoying your Zumba classes with your new mommy friends (by the way, did you know that Zumba was born in Colombia in the '90s? You're welcome, world!) or walking on the treadmill while checking your phone (really?), but it is time to get serious and add weights to your exercise routine. If you use your body weight all the time, your body will get used to it. If you don't have a gym, just buy two sets of dumbbells, leg weights, and/or a resistance band. Using weights builds muscle more effectively than cardio and promotes a boost in metabolism that carries on long after your workout is done. Do not worry about getting bulky. You have to eat a lot to put on size (lots of protein!), so just keep your diet lean.

I know you are busy planning your baby's first birthday party, but do not postpone your workout routine until things get easier, because—I am sorry to tell you this—they won't. I'm going to share a sample routine and some tips that you can do now or in the very near future. Don't let this routine intimidate you. It's just a guide and you can even do it at home in as little as fifteen minutes. In a perfect world, you would work out five to six times a week, but if you can only do three, that's OK. Do what you can (remember that walking with your stroller counts!) and what you enjoy at that moment. I have weeks and even months when I only do gym classes and force myself to stay there for an hour. At other times, I prefer doing my own routine at the gym or at home while I watch TV at night, or I do more stuff outdoors. The most important thing is to mix up your routine and keep moving. It's good for your body and your brain! In her book, *Healthy Brain, Happy Life*, Dr. Wendy Suzuki, a neuroscientist from New York University, discovered that exercise supercharges your brain. When you exercise, your brain actually *performs* better. Basically, you can make yourself smarter! And when you feel stronger, whether it's in a month, six months, or a year, go for heavier weights, more repetitions, longer runs, or shorter breaks when you work out. This can really help you to transform your body.

Sample Routine:
Day 1: Strength Training + Abs
Day 2: Cardio
Day 3: Strength Training + Abs
Day 4: Cardio or Rest
Day 5: Strength Training + Abs
Day 6: Flexibility
Day 7: Rest

* **Strength Training:** Dumbbells and/or a resistance band at home, weight machines and dumbbells at the gym, or use your bodyweight doing squats, lunges (add dumbbells when you are feeling stronger), pushups, and planks at home. A barre class or an intense yoga class. If you are doing two to three days of strength training, try to alternate: one day arms, one day legs and butt. Always finish with a session of abs. My favorite abs workouts are: Stability Ball Jackknives, Planks, Moving Plank Side to Side, and Side Bridge.

* **Cardio:** Running, swimming (it is the perfect workout because it uses nearly every muscle in your body), spinning,

hiking, jump rope (if you were good at this when you were eight years old, you probably still are!), elliptical or treadmill machine at your gym. Aerobics class, Zumba class, or a fast-paced walk with the stroller.

* **Flexibility:** Beginner's yoga or Pilates class or some yoga poses or stretching exercises at home.

Fit Mom Basics

* Breastfeed

* Wear a waist trainer for the first three months

* Do not skip breakfast

* Work out at least three days a week for 30 minutes and go for a stroller walk once a day for at least 30 minutes

* Drink a cup of warm water with lemon first thing in the morning, three to four cups of decaf green tea and plenty of water during the day

* Eat lean protein for lunch and dinner with lots of vegetables, fruit in the morning, stay away from processed foods, snack wisely and watch your portion size

* If you need sweets in your life, choose dark chocolate and no more than once a day

* Go whole wheat (but don't overeat, thinking that just because it's whole wheat you can eat as much as you want). Look for foods made with 100 percent whole grains and go for a variety

* And finally, remember, it is not a diet or a boot camp, it's a lifestyle, and working on yourself will always be the best thing you can do—not only for yourself, but for your family too!

Part Three
Beauty & Style

Some pregnant women focus so much on their growing bellies that they forget to appreciate the thick, shiny hair, strong nails (it was the first time I had long nails), glowing skin, full plump lips, and that lovely natural glow. A couple of months after your baby is born, your hair will be brittle and falling out, your dark circles will be deeper, and there might be some small dark patches on your skin (you know, the ones you try to get closer to the mirror to figure out what the hell it is). Your nails will be weak, and while your breasts might be bigger, so will your feet! (Which is not great for your precious shoe collection.) You check your closet and all you have is maternity clothes (that you're sick of!) or office clothes. (Did I really need that many boring black pants?) If you nodded your head at least twice while reading that, then this chapter is for you! In this section, I'll help you get back to looking your best after your baby is born.

Skincare In 1, 2, 3 … 6

I grew up seeing my mom with a tomato mask on her face and olive oil in her hair every Sunday. When I moved to London, the first letter that I received from her (yes, a letter, not an email. That's how old I am! In my defense, email was already around, but my mom had not figured it out yet) that said: please make sure that you moisturize your skin every day and have a homemade treatment for your hair once a week. This chapter is about what I have learned from the last 15 years. Lots of tried and tested ideas in here.

Even though your skin will be glowing after having a baby, you will be exhausted and it will start to show. Do not worry for the first month. Just make sure that you wash your face and put on moisturizer or an eye cream here and there, whenever you have time. After the second month (or third!), you need to start paying attention to your skin. For many years I thought that it was enough to clean and moisturize my skin. As I get older, my routine has become longer, but not too complicated.

Korean products are taking the beauty industry by storm; even Sephora has a category on their website called Korean beauty. Charlotte Cho mentions 10 steps for the perfect Korean complexion in her book *The Little Book of Skin Care*. Korean beauty is very focused on cleaning your skin. I also like the French approach, which is based on natural ingredients and is very similar to the Colombian approach. I also like the recommendation to exfoliate your skin more than once a week as a key to a great complexion. I do not follow any regimen in particular. I have adapted everything that I have read and learned over the years into my own skincare routine.

After you wake up and feed and change the baby, take three minutes of your time for your skin care routine. The right products are as important as the discipline. If you are very tired one day and you sleep with your makeup on or don't have time to do one step, it is OK. But try to be as consistent as you can and you will see amazing changes in your skin. Also, as busy moms we may not have time to apply much makeup. In order to look decent with minimal makeup, we must have radiant skin. It is difficult for busy sleep-deprived moms, but try to make an effort with your routine. There is no easy solution for skin; you have to work on it daily.

The following steps and overall skin care chapter were reviewed by Dr. Mitchel P. Goldman. He is a world-renowned, double-board certified dermatologist and cosmetic surgeon, recognized by the American Board of Dermatology and the American Board of Cosmetic Surgery. Dr. Goldman is known for pioneering research on multiple laser techniques, skin rejuvenation, liposculpture, and vein therapy.

Morning
1. Cleanse

Cleansing is the most important step in the Korean skincare routine. If your skin is not clean, then your other products won't work, as they cannot be absorbed. Makeup, pollution, and excess sebum sit on the surface of your skin and settle into your pores, which causes acne and can contribute to lines, wrinkles, and uneven pigmentation.

2. Tone

The *French Beauty Solution Book* recommends toning your skin. According to this book, many American women think toners are astringent in nature and meant only for those with oily skin, but actually, they perfect the cleansing step, getting rid of soapy residue, adding moisture to your skin, and preparing your skin for the next step by normalizing the pH. Try a hydrating toning spray with no alcohol. You will be amazed how much makeup or dirt is left on your skin when you think you have removed it all with cleanser. I try to do it every day. If I am in a hurry in the morning, this is the step that I skip, but when I do it, I like how my skin feels afterward.

3. Serum

As this product is lighter and thinner, it penetrates more deeply and quickly into your skin. You will only need a few drops. If you have dark spots after pregnancy, acne scars, or you have freckles like me, the usual recommendation is to use serums with vitamin C, but they can sometimes be very irritating. Look for a serum with a good mix of antioxidants or hyaluronic acid. (More about this ingredient later.) Also, serums can make your sunscreen more effective. Skinceuticals has the best serums with a variety of antioxidants that are not as irritating as vitamin C.

4. Moisturizer

A moisturizer should have a good mix of antioxidants. Those are vitamins, minerals, and enzymes that slow or prevent the oxidation process caused by free radicals. (Think of when a peeled apple or sliced avocado turns brown; that is oxidation.) When free radical damage occurs on the skin, we see more sunspots, freckles, uneven skin tone, fine lines, wrinkles, and even skin cancer. This is why it's important to constantly replenish your supply of antioxidants. Look for moisturizers that have top quality antioxidants such as lycopene, vitamin A, ferulic acid, green tea, resveratrol, or alpha lipoic. The more antioxidants your moisturizer has the better, as they work together for optimal results.

5. Eye cream

The sleepless nights are going to take a toll on you. Try to moisturize the eye area twice a day. Also, apply the cream anywhere you see a line, such as smile and frown lines. Those with hyaluronic acid work best to hydrate the skin.

6. Sunscreen

Sun exposure accelerates skin aging, and yet only 30 percent of women in the U.S. wear sunscreen daily. According to a Harvard Study presented at the American Academy of Dermatology's annual conference in March 2016, women who protect their skin from the sun look up to 20 years younger! More important than drinking water or getting your beauty sleep is keeping out of the sun and wearing sunscreen when this is not possible.

Do not rely on makeup for your SPF protection. Try to go for a mineral-based sunscreen because chemical sunscreens can aggravate sensitive skin. Mineral sunscreens do not interact with the skin, rather, they sit on top of it to block UV rays. Always make sure to use broad spectrum with UVA and UVB protection. Use SPF protection every single day, even in winter. Sunscreens work best when combined with antioxidants; that's why it is a good idea to use the moisturizer first and then your sunblock.

Don't Forget Your Neck and Chest

Include all these steps for your neck and chest too! Your neck and chest need as much attention, if not more, as your face, as skin over this area is thin, has fewer oil glands, and doesn't have much collagen. It can get ugly pretty fast. Using sunblock is very important too.

Useful Tip

It can be difficult to do all six steps when you have your baby with you. I clean and tone after I change my baby. I like to wait a little bit between the serum and the moisturizer to give the skin time to absorb the ingredients. I apply eye cream once we move to the kitchen to make breakfast, since I keep my eye cream in the fridge. If we are going out, I apply the sunblock before we leave. Again, consistency is key. You can skip any step if you are in hurry or your baby isn't having it. But please, never skip the sunscreen if you are leaving the house!

Night

1. **Remove makeup.** When I wear makeup, I cleanse with wipes and then eye makeup remover. Otherwise, I skip this step.

2. **Exfoliate.** I try to do it twice a week with a Clarisonic skin brush. The key to exfoliating is to do it with the right product and not a standard scrub. And yes, we should exfoliate and then clean the skin. As Dr. Lancer explains in his book, *Younger: The Breakthrough Anti-Aging Method for Radiant Skin*, "Say you want to replace a tile floor. If your epidermis is the floor, then exfoliation is the gentle lifting process that breaks up the old, worn-out tiles. Next you have to scoop up and sweep away the debris, the cleanse step in the Lancer Method that washes away exfoliant, excess oil, and dirt." Daily damage, age damage, and sun damage need to be exfoliated before the face is cleansed.

3. **Cleanse.** Use a gentle soap and a Clarisonic brush.

4. **Apply serum.** I like the ones that include hyaluronic acid, which helps with the appearance of aging skin.

5. **Apply retinol.** (if you are not breastfeeding)

6. **Moisturize.** (at night, same as in the morning)

7. **Apply eye cream.** I prefer something heavier at night.

Useful Tip

There are going to be nights that you are so tired that you don't want to even brush your teeth, let alone do all these nighttime skin care steps. If so, at least wash your face with a liquid soap using your fingers and then apply a moisturizer (the richest that you have) all over your face, including your eye area. I like these masks: Glamglow Thirstymud Hydrating Treatment and Kiehl's Ultra Facial Overnight Hydrating Mask; both deliver instant, extreme moisture and you can leave them on all night. They are available at Sephora; ask for a sample to try it first and use it just when needed.

Retinoids Are a Must
(unless you are breastfeeding)

There are two types of retinoids, Retin-A and retinol. Retin-A is a prescription medication and retinol is the milder version, which is available over the counter. If you have ever heard about tretinoin, this is the generic name for Retin-A. Retinol is not as potent as Retin-A, but it can have similar anti-aging effects. If you are applying either of these, do not forget to apply sunscreen during the day, as they make your skin more sensitive to the sun.

Retinol

Retinol is a pure form of vitamin A, which your skin uses naturally in its regeneration and repair cycle, making it the anti-aging ingredient most recommended by dermatologists. The benefits of retinol include a visible reduction in the appearance of wrinkles and dramatic improvements in texture, tone, and radiance. It's even good for acne. Don't think you have to be 50 to start using retinol; it's great for people of any age and the results are cumulative: the longer you use it, the better your skin will look. Be aware though, it is not recommended for women who are pregnant or breastfeeding. If you are new to retinol, start slow, just twice a week and then increase to every other day. Your skin will look a bit irritated and it will peel slightly at the beginning, but this shows that the product is working! Going back to retinol was the thing that I was looking forward to the most when I stopped breastfeeding.

Retin-A

Retin-A is the only cream scientifically proven to tighten skin and reduce fine lines. It is usually more expensive, and is only available with a doctor's prescription in the U.S. This is for more mature skin. You will be fine with retinol.

Please note that there are a variety of concentrations of both retinol and Retin-A starting at 0.01 percent (the weakest), then 0.025, 0.04, 0.05 and finally, 0.1 (the strongest). A good percentage to start with is 0.025. Always check with your dermatologist. The creams can be very irritating and should be used under a physician's guidance.

Hyaluronic acid

Hyaluronic acid is naturally present in the human body and is a skin care star. It hydrates, plumps, and rejuvenates your skin. It penetrates and protects skin for continuous, locked-in moisture due to its varied molecular weight. Every woman should add this to her skincare routine. You will find this ingredient primarily in serums and moisturizers.

If You Have Sensitive Skin…hold on!

If your skin is sensitive, it is better for you not to follow all these steps. Check with your dermatologist to find out the best products for you. You might need prescription products. The best thing to do is use products with as few ingredients as possible. Avoid washing your face with hot water and excessive showering or bathing (the steam from the shower is bad for your face; shower with the door open and with lukewarm water). Harsh exfoliators and homemade treatments should also be avoided. Only use soothing, creamy non-soap cleansers or cleansing oils, and apply moisturizer when the skin is wet to let the hydrators penetrate into the deeper layer of the skin. For sensitive skin anti-aging products, it is better not to use retinol. Look for creams with peptides or hyaluronic acid (again, check with your doctor) and always go for mineral sunblock. I will give you some product recommendations in the next section.

Facial Masks

Once a week or every other week, I do a homemade mask or a sheet mask. Sheet masks have long been a mainstay in Asian skin care. They are not expensive, very effective, and they target specific skin conditions. They hydrate, brighten, and refresh your skin, and are a great way to pamper yourself.

The "Essence" of Beauty

If you are a beauty junkie, you've probably heard of essences. An essence is not a serum or a toner, it's a lightweight, hydrating liquid, designed to help prepare skin for a moisturizer. This is the heart of the Korean skin care routine. For Korean women, this is the most important step and they have amazing skin. It helps to hydrate skin and increase cell turnover.

You should apply it after the toner and before the serum. You can pat it or press it into your face with your hands, starting at your chin and moving upward. If you have oily skin or acne, this product might not be for you.

I use it when I have time, when my skin feels a bit dry or during a long flight. My favorites are: AmorePacific, and Kiehl's essence. The most famous is SK-II, which Cate Blanchett (who has the most amazing skin) swears by.

Melasma

It is very common during and after pregnancy to have melasma, otherwise known as the pregnancy mask (how lovely!). About half of women experience this condition, which usually manifests as dark patches on the forehead, cheeks, or upper lip. It affects all skin tones but is most prevalent in women with a darker complexion.

Melasma is very close to my heart because I had it above my upper lip after having my baby, and it made me look like the female version of Cantinflas. (If you don't know who Cantinflas is, Google it and feel sorry for me. Do not laugh!) To be honest, it was not that bad. My closest friends and my very sincere and ruthless sister said that they could not see it (I never dared to ask my husband). But I did every single thing in the world to get rid of it, and I conquered it.

The first rule for treating melasma is to avoid sun exposure on your face. Heat and sun can aggravate it and even overhead lights at home can make it worse. Wear sunscreen daily, year round, and at least SPF 30 with zinc oxide and/or titanium dioxide. If you are planning a vacation or to spend a lot of time outdoors during the summer, dermatologists recommend avoiding the sun unless you have a large brimmed hat and apply sunblock every two hours. Avoid waxing the areas of the body affected by the condition, which may cause skin inflammation.

To treat it, you can use hydroquinone for deep brightening (if you are not nursing). Although hydroquinone is FDA-approved as a skin lightener in the U.S., it has been banned in parts of Europe and Asia. (The biggest risk of hydroquinone use appears to be the fact that some formulations contain trace amounts of mercury; these formulations were found only in Mexico, Africa, and the Middle East.) If you are using any type of product with hydroquinone, you must use a sunscreen daily, and try to avoid the sun. You should get a prescription from your doctor and follow his recommendations on percentage (usually they recommend 2 percent or 4 percent), length of application (apply daily for eight weeks, three months, or six months, or start using it only twice a week) and frequency (day and night or only night). Do what the doctor says! You need to do your own research and check with your doctor if you want to use this controversial ingredient, which is the most effective ingredient to treat melasma. You will see results in two to three months.

If you are not sure about hydroquinone, vitamin C and licorice are natural options. They slow down the production of melanin, but they do not work as well as hydroquinone. (These two are safe when you are nursing.) You can also use a glycolic acid treatment once or twice a week (low concentration, 10 percent or less). Another option is SkinMedica Lytera 2.0 Pigment Correcting Serum, which relies on a marine extract blend and niacinamide to lighten dark spots without the use of hydroquinone. You can use it if you are breastfeeding, but it takes longer to see results compared with hydroquinone. According to my own research and one recognized dermatologist based in Houston, it works better on Caucasian skin. If your skin is sensitive, Caudalie Vinoperfect Radiance Serum is a great option. A new hydroquinone free product with promising results is Skinceuticals Discoloration Defense Serum. Always check these products with your dermatologist to make sure that they are right for you. For homemade treatments, read the next chapter. After childbirth, or when a woman stops taking birth control, melasma can fade. However, if it does not go away or you want to keep taking birth control pills, you can see a dermatologist to discuss the right treatments for you. The longer you have a melasma patch without treating, the harder it is to fade.

More Tools to Treat your Melasma

* Heliocare: These are vegetarian capsules that help maintain the skin's ability to protect itself against sun-related damage. They are great to take every day, during the summer, or when you are going to a sunny destination. But you still need to wear sunblock!

* ColoreScience Sunforgettable Brush-on SPF 50 UVA/UVB. This is a touch-up sunscreen that looks like a portable blush brush. As you need to apply sunscreen several times during the day, you can apply this one over your makeup and it works as a finishing powder, too. (I always keep mine in my car.)

Make an Appointment with a Dermatologist

I know that we get very busy and the last thing we want to do is go for a doctor's appointment that isn't urgent. You would think that skin-related problems such as melasma, acne, red patches, or surgery scars would heal on their own, but one appointment with your doctor can save you time and worry, giving you the right treatment or product. Nine months after having my baby, I had acne on my forehead for three months and I just could not be bothered to go to the doctor. I kept thinking, next week it will be better ... until I finally made the time to go. He gave me a prescription for one product and after two weeks, my face was clear.

Product Recommendations

By the time this book is out, there will be new products on the market, but the list below contains a variety of products that have worked really well for me. Some that dermatologists have recommended to me over the years, others I found in skin care books and tried, and have been part of the Best Beauty Buys for several years in beauty magazines.

Daytime:

Cleanse

* Neutrogena Naturals Purifying Facial Cleanser

* Caudalie Instant Foaming Cleanser Grapes & Sage

* Kiehl's Ultra Facial Cleanser (my favorite)

* Kiehl's Midnight Recovery Botanical Cleansing Oil (if you're looking for an oil-based cleanser)

Tone

* Burt's Bees Rosewater Toner

* Fresh Rose Floral Toner

* Caudalie Moisturizing Toner Concentrate Vinolevure

Serum

* Olay Regenerist Regenerating Serum

* Ole Henriksen Truth Serum

* SkinCeuticals Phloretin CF Gel (normal, dry, or oily)

* SkinCeuticals C E Ferulic (normal, dry, or sensitive)

* These last two from SkinCeuticals are expensive but highly recommended and should be only used in the morning.

Moisturizers

* Simple Nourishing 24 Hour Day and Night Cream (great for sensitive skin)

* Dermalogica Dynamic Skin Recovery

* Kiehl's Super Multi-Corrective Cream

* SkinMedica Replenish Hydrating Cream (this one has a great mix of antioxidants)

Eye Cream

* Olay Illuminating Eye Cream

* Origins Ginzing Refreshing Eye Cream (best for dark circles and puffy eyes)

* Bioderma Sensibio Eye Contour Gel (sensitive skin)

* Kiehl's Powerful-Strength Line-Reducing Eye-Brightening Concentrate (you must use another eye cream on top of it as this serum isn't moisturizing enough on its own. Any under-eye cream is fine. I know it is a bit of a hassle, but this eye serum really delivers!)

* SkinCeutical AOX Eye Gel

Sunscreen

* Neutrogena Sheer Zinc Face

* My favorite is Le Roche-Posay Anthelios 50 Mineral Tinted Ultra-Light Sunscreen Fluid. (If your skin is oily, try Le Roche-Posay Anthelios 60 shield Dry Touch, which keeps shine at bay and excess oil production to a minimum. I love the tinted version. Its shade goes with every skin tone. If you are not wearing makeup, this will give you a subtle color; just apply blush afterwards.)

* SkinMedica Defense + Repair SPF 50+ (It's great if you live in a hot and humid city or spend too much time in the sun. It is the first sunscreen to block infrared radiation.)

Nighttime:
Makeup Removal

* Burt's Bees Facial Cleansing Towelettes with White Tea

* Garnier Skin Active Micellar (This cleansing water does really remove all your makeup including your mascara, and it's great for sensitive skin.)

* Neutrogena Oil-Free Eye Makeup Remover, or Almond Oil or Jojoba Oil

Exfoliator

* Dermalogica Multivitamin Thermafoliant

* Philosophy The Microdelivery Exfoliating Wash

* Amore Pacific Treatment Enzyme Peel Botanical Exfoliator (I love this product. It is a bit expensive but worth it. It is the kind of exfoliator that you can even use every day. One bottle will last you up to a year.)

Night Moisturizers

* Same as the morning moisturizers.

Retinol

* Neutrogena Rapid Wrinkle Repair Moisturizer (this one is loved by dermatologists)

* Dermalogica Retinol Repair 1%

* SkinMedica Retinol Complex .25

For the last two, a consultation with your dermatologist is recommended, as the creams can be irritating.

Facial Mask

* Kiehl's Rare Earth Pore Cleansing Masque (Oily skin and large pores)

* Kiehl's Turmeric & Cranberry Seed Energizing Radiance Mask (Dullness and uneven texture)

* REN Glycol Lactic Radiance Renewal Mask (Uneven skin tone, fine lines and wrinkles)

* Glam Glow Youthmud Tinglexfoliate Treatment (Dullness, fine lines, and large pores)

Hyaluronic Acid

* Neutrogena Hydro Boost Hydrating Serum

* SkinCeuticals Hyaluronic Acid Intensifier

Sheet masks

* Garnier SkinActive Moisture Bomb

* Dr. Jart + Water Replenishment Cotton Sheet Mask

Acne Treatment

* Kate Somerville EradiKate (The one and only!)

Sephora sales

You can find most of these products at CVS, Target, and Sephora. Remember that Sephora offers discounts in April after Easter and just before Thanksgiving, so those are great times to stock up on the most expensive products.

Going Organic?

If you are looking for an organic skin care company, Juice Beauty is a great option. They only use certified organic ingredients without potentially harmful ingredients. Their makeup (plant-pigment) products are great, too. You can find this brand at Whole Foods and Ulta. My favorite products are:

* Cleansing Milk Daily, Essentials Skincare

* Green Apple Age Defy Organic Serum, Brightening Skincare

* Stem Cellular Resurfacing Micro-Exfoliant, Anti-Wrinkle Moisturizer, Booster Serum and Eye Treatment, Anti-Wrinkle Skincare.

Express Facial at Home

When your baby goes to bed on time and is sleeping through the night (or for a couple of hours straight), treat yourself to this facial:

* Remove makeup

* Exfoliate with the Clarisonic device

* Boil water in a lidded pot on the stove; add lavender oil if you want

* Take the lid off, put a towel over your head, lean over the pot, inhale, and relax for five minutes. Do not put your face too close to the water

* Wash your face with soap or a cleanser to remove any sweat

* If you have any pimples, try to squeeze them very gently with your fingers wrapped in paper. If you don't get anything, do not try again, just leave it. I know, it's so difficult to leave it alone!

* Put on a face mask, preferably one with natural ingredients and leave it for fifteen minutes.

* Remove it with a wet, warm clean cloth

* Apply a thick moisturizer

* Apply eye cream
* Seal your pores with spray water (rosewater if you have it) and tap your fingers lightly over your skin

The Beauty Tool Must-Have for Every Mom

A Clarisonic brush! If you don't own one, find a way to get one. Save up for one or ask for it as a present for your birthday or anniversary, for Christmas, or for International Women's Day (it's March 8, by the way). Just find an excuse. There are cheaper versions, but they are too harsh and this one will last you a long time. The Clarisonic skin brush uses ultrasonic energy to clean your skin, removing environmental pollutants, as well as dirt and oil from your pores. I recommended this device to a friend of mine (plus retinol) and after three months, I could tell the difference in her skin.

Spa facials

Sometimes, going to a spa for a nice massage or a facial can be just what we need. I love going to my local spa for a facial two or three times per year, usually one before spring, another around my birthday (just in case I get some spots), and one before the December holidays. Ask your spa if they do a shorter version of their signature facial. It will be cheaper! If you are over 30 and have the financial means, consider starting with something more "hardcore" for your face. I am not suggesting fillers or Botox. Check with your dermatologist or spa about laser therapy (if they have doctors or certified nurses), ultrasonic treatment, microdermabrasion, or peels (I am not a big fan of peels, but some experts recommend them; check with your dermatologist). They will help you with fine lines and sun damage and stimulate the production of collagen and elastin in your skin.

Body Care

When I lived in London, the first house that I lived in was with a group of Brazilian women "meninas" (which means "girls" in Portuguese). I was the only Colombian in the house—and the only one who took a shower in the morning. We all worked as waitresses in luxury hotels and started work very early in the morning. I remember seeing them going to have a shower at night. I thought it was so weird that I even told my friends back in Colombia. Can you believe this? They also shower at night! I don't understand. I felt bad that I was the only one showering just one time a day. Then I found out that they only shower at night; the next day they only washed their faces, had breakfast, and were ready to go to work. After having my baby, when I had crazy mornings and quiet nights, I started showering at night. I am officially a menina! I can see the benefits now: I go to my sanctuary bed all clean, and I do not have to rush or open the shower door every minute to make sure that my baby is not crying after I put him down for a nap. It helps me to relax at night, and unless the baby awakens unexpectedly, I can follow my beauty routine without interruptions. I like showering with the lights off and just my small makeup mirror light on. I dry brush my skin before I shower. I also prepare a very hot cup of herbal tea first and drink it when I get out, while I apply my beauty products.

As I have said many times, consistency is key. I also understand that sometimes we are too tired to go through the whole regimen or even take a shower. And yes, this has happened to me many times! That said, these are the products I apply at night:

Legs, arms, and tummy. Jojoba, almond, or avocado oil (Whole Foods has a good selection). I also like The Honest Company Organic Body Oil.

Thighs and butt. Weleda Birch Cellulite Oil. It really worked for me and the smell is very fresh. Because of its natural ingredients, it is OK to use while pregnant or breastfeeding. If you are not breastfeeding, Finulite (on Amazon) is great for cellulite. It comes with a cream for day and night. I have tried all the creams for cellulite and this one always delivers.

Breasts. Organic Evening Primrose Oil. According to the book, *Bio Young* by Roxy Dillon, who has practiced nutritional, orthomolecular, and herbal therapy since 1979 "It increases breast size by increasing fat and glandular tissue in this area and thus lends bounce and lift". As a formerly perky 34B who breastfed for one year, I really want to believe this, but I have not seen "bigger" changes. At least I am moisturizing this area (very sad consolation). Honey is also supposed to result in fuller and firmer breasts. Just apply it when you are showering and leave it on for a few minutes.

This routine may sound like it takes forever but it actually takes only seven minutes (including my skin care routine). This is probably less time than the average person spends on social media every night.

The Secret to Soft Hands

My nails are very weak and short and my cuticles are always dry. I used to buy expensive hand creams, thinking the best ingredients would help. One day I decided to put my baby's Aquaphor cream on my hands and nails just before going to bed. The next day my hands felt great. It contains vitamin D, which is healing, particularly for winter skin. It works great on your feet, too! Slip on a pair of cotton socks after you apply to hold in moisture.

I like The Honest Company Healing Balm, too, but any cream that you are using for your baby would be good for your hands and your feet.

Even though this might not be your biggest concern right now, remember that our hands show our age more than any other part of our body. The hands take a lot of abuse and most women neglect them when performing their beauty routines. The skin on your hands is just as delicate as the skin around your eyes. Try to moisturize them every time you wash your hands, or at least before you go to bed. When you drive, apply sunblock on your hands before you take the wheel. I always have a stick sunblock in the center console; a cream would be too messy.

Stretch Marks—Can They Be Avoided?

If you are pregnant and reading this book...

The best way to avoid stretch marks during pregnancy is to "swim" in oil twice a day. This works better than body lotion or creamand you don't have to spend a lot of money. I used both expensive brands and drugstore brands, and I did not get any stretch marks. I already had some stretch marks on my butt after my teenage years, so I was concerned I would get them during pregnancy, but this kept them away. I prefer to go for something fragrance-free and natural with organic ingredients when possible. Apply it on your belly as well as your hips, breasts, arms, and waist. You can even get stretch marks on the backs of your knees. Apply it everywhere. This is why I say "swim" in oil. These are my recommendations:

* Palmer's Cocoa Butter Formula with Vitamin E Skin Therapy Oil
* Bio Oil
* Earth Mama Angel Baby Natural Stretch Oil
* Mama Mio The Tummy Rub Oil
* Elemis Japanese Camellia Oil Blend

Too Late, I Already Have Them

OK, breathe. Unfortunately, there is not much you can do. If they are still red you can treat them with lasers, but it is very expensive—about \$2,000 for three sessions—and it won't make them completely disappear.

I have tried several creams to treat my old stretch marks and my favorite is Body Merry Stretch Marks and Scars. (Available on Amazon, where else?) Its organic ingredients, plant oils, and vitamins really deliver. Your stretch marks won't disappear, but they will be less noticeable. Apply it twice a day. Applying any leftover retinol that is on your hands when you put it on your face at night may help as well.

What about Cellulite?

I have been obsessed with how to cure cellulite since the first time that I saw it on my thighs when I was a 23 living on frozen dinners and highly processed ready-made meals in London. I have gotten rid of it several times, and I was even cellulite-free after I had my baby. But if you let yourself go just a little, especially after 30—weekend pizza for a whole month, not going to the gym in the winter, or even just a couple of cheese sticks (OK, lots)—there it is again.

I could write a whole book on this subject but I am going to be very straightforward. We have bigger worries now! If you really want to get rid of cellulite, the steps below will help, but it takes a big commitment. And remember, a couple of dimples here and there that are visible only when you wear a swimsuit is not a big deal. Everyone is looking at your cute baby, not at your cellulite!

1. Drybrush in the morning and at night. If you don't know what this is, it is exactly what it sounds like: brushing your dry skin with a dry brush. You are supposed to start at your feet in a circular motion and work your way up your body, even in areas where you don't have cellulite, to stimulate lymph flow and improve detoxification. But I only do this on my cellulite problem areas. Be gentle! I like The Body Shop body brushes.

2. Drink water with lemon first thing in the morning. Add one tablespoon of apple cider vinegar, which is great at flushing out toxins and

water retention around the thighs. It even helps you lose those unwanted pounds. Make sure that you buy unfiltered vinegar made from ripe organic apples to ensure that it contains the raw enzymes and beneficial bacteria that are responsible for the majority of its benefits. If you want to go crazy, add cayenne pepper, as it can help get rid of toxins and dead skin cells and replace them with strong, healthy cells. Repeat at night. Does it taste good? Of course not. But you want to get rid of cellulite, right?

3. Cut processed meat from your diet.

4. Do squats and forward and reverse lunges. Add weights, or even better, a kettlebell. Kettlebells demand the use of multiple muscle groups, burning fat and building muscle more quickly, and when there is more muscle than fat, cellulite is less likely to occur.

5. Drink plenty of water.

6. Apply cellulite cream morning and night.

7. Wash with seaweed soap. Seaweed stimulates blood circulation, improves skin texture, and flushes harmful toxins from the body. I recommend The Seaweed Bath Co. Detox Cellulite Bar Soap (Amazon and Target), which also includes arabica coffee, a key ingredient in fighting cellulite.

Good luck! If you feel self-conscious because of your cellulite, try Sally Hansen's Airbrush Legs. This body makeup covers imperfections, evens out your skin tone, and gives you a subtle glow. Then you can just wash it off. Make sure that you have the right shade for your skin, otherwise it can look very fake.

Lose Stress, Not Your Hair

Unlike many women, my hair did not fall out after my pregnancy. People say that this will happen after month five. My birthday was five months after my baby was born, and I thought I was going to celebrate it bald or with a mom bob. But this, thank God, did not happen! I attributed it to several factors:

I only washed my hair twice a week. (Not because I wanted to, I just didn't have the time!)

I kept taking my prenatal vitamins

Every time I washed my hair, I used a homemade treatment that I left on for at least thirty minutes before I washed it.

I barely used any hot tools, such as a flat iron or the curling iron.

I didn't dry my hair straight after showering. I let it air dry as much as I could and then I did a light blow dry.

I took breaks from using my hair dryer for two weeks at a time, periodically.

I had a filter for my shower head.

I used an invisibobble hair tie (Amazon or Sephora), which doesn't crease your hair when you tie it. It also prevents split ends and it doesn't rip your hair out when you remove it.

Hair loss 911

If you suffer from hair loss, there are several essential oils that very effectively stimulate the scalp for hair growth. Eucalyptus globulus increases ceramides in your hair to boost moisture and shine. Recent research has shown that rosemary can stimulate hair follicles to regrow hair. According to Roxy Dillon in her book *Bio Young*, rosemary and eucalyptus are very effective, individually or together, you just rub them into your scalp every night and ou can see results in as little as three weeks. (If you are breastfeeding, it's better not to do this treatment.) It's best to apply the oil every day for the first six months or so. After that, you can skip a day or two, but don't go more than three days between treatments. If your skin is sensitive, you could have some breakouts. (This happened to me and it took me a while to figure out that it was the oil I was putting on my hair, duh!) If this happens to you, simply dilute the oils in a base of olive oil. Use 50 drops each of rosemary and eucalyptus to 100 ml of olive oil. If this still causes a problem, try using just 30 drops each of the essential oils, or even 15 each. Do this before you shampoo, leaving the oils on your scalp for as long as possible, but at least half an hour. If your skin can not tolerate the oils or you find the smell to be too strong, you can try rosemary water. (Instructions in the homemade treatment section.)

It Starts in the Shower

About a year after I moved to the U.S., I noticed that my hair was very dry and tangled. I tried the best shampoos and expensive hair masks. I tried cutting some inches off my hair and washing it with cold water instead of hot. One day my hairdresser asked me if I had changed the filter on my shower head recently. Was I supposed to have a filter? I did not know! Tap water contains chlorine, iron, and rust particles from steel pipes, which can ruin your hair. It strips the shaft of natural oils and dries it out, leaving you with brittle, split ends. It can also affect the color of your hair and leave it brassy. If you feel that I just described your hair, I recommend Jonathan Product Beauty Shower Purification System (Amazon, of course) and make sure to change the filter every six to nine months. Your skin will feel nicer, too.

Shampoo, Conditioner, and Treatment Recommendations

* Pantene Pro-V Daily Moisture Renewal Shampoo and Conditioner

* Garnier Shampoo and Conditioner: Sleek & Shine, Triple Nutrition or Damage Eraser

* Briogeo Rosarco Repair Shampoo and Conditioner

* Kerastase Reflection Bain Chromatique Riche Shampoo and mask (color-treated hair)

* Alterna Haircare Caviar Anti-Aging Replenishing Moisture Shampoo and Conditioner

* Alterna Haircare Caviar Anti-Aging Omega + Nourishing Hair Oil (for dry ends; I apply it after washing my hair)

* Alterna Bamboo Smooth Kendi Oil Pure Treatment Oil (for when my ends feel dry between washes)

* Alterna Haircare Caviar CC Cream for Hair 10-in-1 (I use it as styling cream)

* Kérastase Resistance Serum Therapiste (for very dry and damaged hair, it works!)

Dry Shampoo

* Clean Freak Refreshing Dry Shampoo, Not Your Mother's (drugstore)

* Klorane Dry Shampoo with Oat Milk

Baby hair

I am not talking about your precious baby's hair, but the annoying, extremely curly hair that starts to grow on the front of your hairline the year after you have your baby and makes you want to wear a baseball cap every day. First of all, be grateful—this is new hair that is growing. Nature is beautiful. Second, follow the recommendation of my sister, who, when she saw me with my "new look," desperately licked her hand and passed it through my not-so-sexy curls. Try a Keratin treatment on just your baby hair. Any respected hair salon should offer this treatment. Just make sure that it is formaldehyde free (this ingredient can be carcinogenic). Keratin Complex Smoothing Therapy is a good option. This treatment won't straighten your hair, but it will reduce frizz, curl, and unruly flyaways. Plus your hair will look more put together and daily styling will be easier and quicker. It lasts about three to five months. Even though experts say that this does not damage your hair, I would not recommend doing it more than twice a year and not to all of your hair unless it's very curly and you prefer a more-manageable look. Check with your doctor before doing this treatment if you are nursing.

Bring Back that Fabulous Color

You have highlights and after a couple of months or even weeks (no fair!), your hair is suddenly strawberry orange. After your regular shampoo, apply an anti-yellowing cream, like L'Oréal Color Corrector Blondes and leave it in for ten minutes. It is safe for breastfeeding moms. I also like Kérastase's Reflection Masque Chromatique, which I mix with Kérastase Reflection Touche Chromatique. This is a color-correcting pen and it is available in four shades (I use 'Cool Blonde'). But you need to use it with the mask.

Let's Go to the Bar!

If I have a party to attend or am meeting with friends that I haven't seen for a while, I go to a blow-dry bar, a salon that offers only a blow-out service. Washing and drying my long hair takes a long time and is the thing I like least about getting ready to go out. Even if you don't have great makeup or a trendy outfit, if you have your hair done, you feel like a million bucks! There are some places that offer discounts on certain days of the week or have membership or points packages. Sign up for their discount alerts, too. And yes, I take my baby with me. I have a blow-dry bar in my neighborhood. I take my baby for a stroller walk 30 minutes before my appointment (which I try to make during his naptime) so that my baby sleeps while someone does my hair (the hair dryer is like a white noise machine; brilliant!) If your baby wakes up in the middle of the appointment, just breastfeed or give him a bottle. Problem solved.

The Secret of Eternal Youth

I am not a big fan of big makeovers. One of the keys to looking younger over the years is to maintain the same look (hair length and color.) When you do something drastic, you start looking older. Even TV presenters wear the same lipstick color over the years. You don't have to go to this extreme, but think of Jennifer Aniston, Sofia Vergara, Elle Macpherson, and Christie Brinkley. They look the same as ten or fifteen years ago because they have kept the same hairstyle. If you are happy with your look, don't change it, just go a bit darker or brighter on color and keep close to the same hair length. I like to keep it brighter and a bit shorter in the summer, as it gets very dry, then I go longer than usual with fewer highlights in winter, but overall it looks the same.

Finally, remember that great skin and hair come from within, which is why a healthy and balanced diet is so important.

Homemade Treatments

Now that you are spending so much time at home, you should take advantage of some natural home treatments. Your skin can look smoother and brighter and your hair fuller and shinier with only a few regular kitchen ingredients. Thanks to my mom, my sister and I have had kitchen ingredients in our hair since we were about ten years old. I used to have lard treatments—lard is pig fat for those of you who don't know; yes, pig fat—on my hair on Sunday mornings. I've even had petroleum and vinegar on my hair to make it shiny. I stopped with all-natural ingredients when I moved to London (who has time for that?) but my sister and my mom continued with their homemade concoctions. I can tell you that my sister has long, full, healthy-looking hair and my mom looks ten to fifteen years younger than she actually is. (I would never tell you how old my mom is; I have been trained since I was seven years old to never reveal her age.) Since I am spending more time at home with my baby, I have returned to a more natural approach to beauty. This is what my mom, my sister and I have tried. It works!

Face Time

For your face, let's just start with the Holy Grail ingredient from your kitchen: Honey, honey!

Honey is the best beauty product that you can find in your kitchen. It is a gentle exfoliator and has antibacterial properties that help reduce acne. It treats irritated and sunburned skin and fades scars. Best of all, honey reverses the effects of aging. It contains natural hormones that plump up your skin and restore the deeper layer. You can use it not only on your face, but also your arms, breasts, knees, elbows, and hair. I always have one pot by my shower. Be sure to use raw organic honey to ensure you're getting all the enzymes, antioxidants, and nutrients for your skin will absorb. It is good internally, too. Have two spoons daily. (Unless you are diabetic, of course!)

Smoothing Mask

2 tablespoons of full-fat Greek yogurt

1 teaspoon of raw honey

1 tablespoon of organic oat flour (you can ground the oats into a flour in a food processor)

Mix the ingredients and blend well. Apply to clean skin. Leave the mask on for fifteen minutes. Remove with a warm, damp washcloth. The lactose in the yogurt will help dissolve dead skin cells, the honey will keep moisture close to the skin, and the oats will add serious exfoliation. This mask will leave your skin soft and refreshed!

Anti-Aging Mask

Tomatoes are rich in vitamins A and C, which improve the collagen and elastin production in the skin and give you a glowing complexion. They also slow down the aging process of your skin. This mask is perfect for dry skin.

1 medium tomato smashed with a fork

1 teaspoon milk

1 teaspoon honey

1 tablespoon of ground flaxseed meal or oatmeal (add it for deeper exfoliation)

Blend all the ingredients until the mixture is pureed and smooth. Apply the mask on your face and let it sit for fifteen minutes. Rinse with warm water.

Mask for Oily and Acne-Prone Skin

After honey, strawberries are one of the best natural ingredients for your skin. They are loaded with vitamin C; salicylic acid, which is used in products to treat acne; and alpha-hydroxy acids, which help to exfoliate the skin. Lemon juice is a natural astringent, has antibacterial properties, and can be used to fade acne scars.

2–3 mashed strawberries
1 teaspoon lemon juice
1 teaspoon honey

Apply it on your clean face for ten to fifteen minutes, and then rinse.

Lip Scrub

1 tablespoon of coconut oil (the solid portion)
1 tablespoon of honey
1 teaspoon of brown sugar

Mix the coconut oil with the honey until clump free, then add the sugar and blend well. Add a couple of drops of Jojoba Oil if you have some. Wait for about ten minutes before using it the first time to let the sugar dissolve a bit. Gently scrub your lips in a circular motion. Leave it on for a couple of minutes and then remove it with a warm washcloth. Keep it in the fridge for up to two weeks.

Banana peel

Banana peel! According to leading plastic surgeon Dr. Anthony Youn, in his book "The Age Fix," banana peel works well to treat mild acne. Just rub the inside of the peel onto areas you have acne until the inside of the peel turns brown. Allow the banana residue to dry on your face and leave it for 30 minutes. The banana peel contains fatty acids and antioxidants that soothe the skin. I have tried it and it works!

Egg

Eggs are not only delicious, filling, healthy, and easy to cook, they are also great for your eyes. When you are cooking eggs, take the white part left in the shell and put it around your eyes and smile lines. The egg has a shrink-wrap effect on the face and also reduces the inflammation around the eyes. Leave it on while you're at home, just don't forget to wash it off when you leave the house!

Top Ingredients for Treating Melasma

Before you begin any home treatment for this condition, see a dermatologist to determine whether the dark spots on your skin are caused by melasma.

Aloe Vera

Aloe vera gel contains mucilaginous polysaccharides that lighten blemishes and dark spots caused by excessive sun exposure, and melasma discoloration. Cut open an aloe vera leaf (you can get an aloe vera plant at the grocery store) and extract the fresh gel. Get aloe on fingertips and massage the affected area and then leave it for at least 30 minutes. Do it daily until the spots fade. Aloe vera is excellent for acne, too.

Lemon Juice

The high acidity of lemon juice can help exfoliate the top layer of the skin, and therefore lighten the dark patches. Dip a cotton ball into the juice of a half squeezed lemon, then apply to clean skin where you have melasma spots. Add an equal amount of water to dilute the juice if you have sensitive skin. Leave it on for 20 minutes then rinse it off with lukewarm water. Apply moisturizer, as lemon can be very drying. Since the juice makes your skin hypersensitive to sunlight, only do this treatment at night. If you do it every night, you should see results after two weeks.

Turmeric

Turmeric is an Indian spice that has been used as an ancient remedy to heal and regenerate the skin. Curcumin, its active ingredient, has skin lightening and anti-inflammatory, antibacterial (it can treat pimples and acne), and anti-oxidant properties.

Make a thick paste by mixing two tablespoons of turmeric with four tablespoons of milk or plain yogurt. The turmeric can stain your skin a slight yellow, but this should wear off quickly. Apply this paste on the skin affected by hyperpigmentation and let it dry for 20 minutes. Rinse your skin with lukewarm water while massaging gently in a circular motion. Repeat this treatment daily for best results.

Tomato Paste

Apply tomato paste on the skin affected by hyperpigmentation and let it dry completely. Then rinse your skin with lukewarm water while massaging gently in a circular motion. Repeat daily for best results. Tomato paste also works great in minimizing large pores; apply a thin layer and rinse after five minutes.

Tips

Do facial steam whenever you can before applying a mask. I know finding the time to apply a mask is hard enough, but this will open your pores and let the mask penetrate deeply.

To avoid irritations and even rashes, try to use organic (fruit, vegetables and milk), full fat organic unsweetened yogurt and milk, cold-pressed organic oils and raw honey.

The two top natural ingredients for your skin are honey and yogurt, and both are great bases for your homemade masks. You can mix them with others that you have in your kitchen or what-ever is in season like papaya (great exfoliant), avocado (dry skin), strawberries (oily and acne-prone or uneven skin tone), kiwi (oily skin), pumpkin (dry skin), mango (dry or combination skin and anti-aging), orange and lemon (exfoliation and new cell growth) or banana (for all skin types).

I apply a homemade mask only once a week, as I prefer to make a fresh batch every time. Some ingredients can go bad very quickly. If you're left with excess face mask mixture, use it on your hands, neck, and cleavage before a shower.

I have never had an allergic reaction to a natural treatment. Perhaps because I have been using it since I was 10 years old! But before trying a homemade mask, do a spot test on your neck or your hand to make sure that you do not have an allergic reaction. And of course, if you know you react to any of the ingredients when you eat them, do not put them on your face

Hair Care

Olive oil. Fatty acids and vitamin E make olive oil the perfect at-home hair treatment. Use warm olive oil (heat it slightly) for your split ends. Leave it for 20 - 30 minutes. My sister—the one with the amazing hair—religiously puts olive oil in her hair. This works great for your nails and cuticles, too.

Coconut oil. Also contains proteins that can strengthen your hair and prevent damage. It leaves your hair soft and shiny. Leave it on between 20-30 minutes.

Avocado. They are high in vitamins B and E, which work to protect, moisturize, and strengthen hair and contribute to its growth. I like to mix it with olive oil. Leave it for at least 30 minutes. If your hair is very dry, you can apply it to all of your hair; otherwise, only use it on the ends. Avocado oil is good, too.

Mayonnaise. Yes, you have read correctly, full-fat mayonnaise. Before you say something, this is Blake Lively's natural treatment hair secret. Apply it only on your hair ends for at least 30 minutes.

Rosemary. Boil two cups of water with some rosemary, leave it for ten minutes. Filter the rosemary out and rinse your hair with the rosemary water. It adds shine and it helps hair to grow more quickly. You could also put the rosemary water in a spray bottle and apply to your roots before bed every night. My sister does that!

If you are staying at home, cover your hair with a shower cap or plastic wrap and leave the treatments on for 30 minutes. If I am going for a walk or exercise in the morning, I put olive oil or coconut oil on the ends of my hair and throw on a baseball cap.

Go to the Gym and...Relax?

On most Sundays, I go to my gym. Before heading out, I put some olive oil on the ends of my hair and pack all my beauty products and a book. When I arrive, I do some stretches or light exercise. After that, I go to the steam room. I bring a Ziploc bag with olive oil, brown sugar, and honey to exfoliate my whole body. I stay there for ten to fifteen minutes. Then I shower and wash my hair. I apply oil to my skin while it's still damp and wear something comfy. Then I go to the library (close to my home) or the gym lounge and read for an hour while I drink a big bottle of water. I arrive home feeling very refreshed. Even if you don't have kids, you should do this! If you don't have a gym membership, ask a friend to invite you as a guest. Ask your husband for two hours of his time or get someone to look after the baby for just a couple of hours.

Makeup vs Natural and Everything in Between

After making sure that you have perfect glowing skin by following all the steps for the skin regimen, you can use some basic products for natural looking makeup. The current trend in makeup is the "no-makeup look," but even if it goes out of fashion, it is still perfect for busy new moms. Who has time for contouring? Be sure to check your makeup in natural light, not just the bathroom, because it can look completely different under different lighting. The mirror in your car counts; not when you're in motion, of course.

Base. By now you should know if you are more of a foundation or powder girl. I used to be a Chanel foundation girl in my "sales executive days." Now I don't have the budget or the time to apply and blend it, and I feel that it looks too heavy on me anyway. I have discovered Cushion Compacts, which are lightweight, glow-inducing liquid foundations that create a more natural look. They were developed in Seoul, South Korea, in 2007 and it is estimated that an IOPE Air Cushion XP (the original) is sold every six seconds in that mega city. I really like the one L'Oréal makes; you can apply it on the go, it has its own cushion, so you don't get messy fingers, and it blends easily. It runs out fast though, which is why I like to buy a drugstore version. If you have a bigger budget, Amore

Pacific (Sephora) is a great option. Its potent Asian botanicals deeply hydrate the skin. Other easy-to-apply natural options are tinted moisturizers or tinted BB creams.

What are BB creams? BB is a blemish balm or base which does the job of a moisturizer, primer, sunscreen, skin treatment, concealer, and foundation. All in one product! Personally, I do not use a BB cream on a daily basis, as I always prefer to apply foundation and sunscreen separately, but if I'm in a rush, this is what I use. To broaden your knowledge in beauty products (now that you are an expert on diaper creams), there is also a CC cream (color or correcting cream) that goes on a little more sheer and has a more natural look.

After using tinted moisturizer, BB cream, or CC cushion, you can skip the powder (if your skin is not oily). For summer, I like to apply bronzer instead of powder. (I prefer a version with no shimmer).

When you are applying your base, blend well at the edges to avoid a visible line.

Pro tip. Whether using foundation or powder, for a more natural look, do not cover your nose. If you are using the cushion for a more natural look, you don't need to blend it to the neck, just a bit of bronzer (without shimmer) on the neck will do.

Concealer. If cleansing and sunblock are the foundation for radiant skin, concealer is the key to looking decent and being accepted by society, to be dramatic. Even if you don't have dark circles you will benefit from it. If you use foundation, BB cream, tinted moisturizer, or a Cushion Compact (which I highly recommend!), the concealer goes on after, and if you use powder it goes before. Just make sure that you have applied an eye cream before so the concealer will blend easily and won't look cakey. Always blend it with your small finger to put less pressure on your face. For melasma patches, use a peachy tone to neutralize the dark color and don't rub it. Just tap the melasma spot with your index finger once or twice and apply a bit of your base after.

Makeup vs Natural and Everything in Between

Cheeks. Most women say that they cannot live without mascara. I cannot live without blush. Sometimes, if I don't have time to apply my Cushion Compact, I apply blush. If you follow the steps for radiant skin, that may be all you need (OK, and mascara, too!) Don't smile as you apply blush to the apples of your cheeks, as the color will end up on the lower part of your face.

The "no-makeup" look goes for highlighter on the cheeks instead of blush, which I really like for a more natural look or when I have the time to define my eyes for an important occasion. If you prefer this technique, go easy on the highlighter.

If you have extra time... Add highlighter on the top of your cheekbones and the bridge of your nose. I just apply powder vertically along the center of the nose with my finger. If you want to slim your nose, apply a bronzer (without shimmer) or shadow two shades darker than your normal skin color along the sides of your nose; gently blend and apply powder to set. (Make sure that you do not powder the front of your nose, only the corners). For a night out, apply bronzer under your cheeks. OK, yes, all of this is contouring!

Brows. They are the frame of your face. Try to keep them trimmed. As you won't be using too much makeup, having clean eyebrows is important. I go once every two months to have them waxed (and pluck to maintain them between visits). Set and define your brows with clear or tinted brow gel. If you've never had your eyebrows done (Seriously? Please do. It is a life changer), try Anastasia Brow Studio at Nordstrom. Anastasia is the queen of brows in Hollywood and the founder of the cosmetic brand Anastasia Beverly Hills. Her brow studio experts use the Anastasia method, which is wax and tweeze.

If you have extra time... Get the perfect brow color and fill in spaces with a brow powder (wet the brush a bit) and brow brush.

Eyes. Let's just keep it simple: eyelash curler and mascara. Nothing else. Do not apply foundation or an eye base to your lids, because if you don't apply eyeshadow afterward, it will look cakey. And please do not use white shadow underneath the brow. This technique is from 2003. Since I use castor oil every night, I have long lashes (I wanted to give you this tip before, but I thought it was too much, so here you have it), so I just use the eyelash curler. But you can apply mascara or a clear gel (if you do not want to be bothered with taking the mascara off at night) after using the curler.

If you have extra time... Apply a semi-dark brown shade along and just above the upper and lower lash line. If you're feeling more adventurous, underline the lower lash line with a dark nude lip pencil (yes, a lip pencil) starting from the middle and going outward. For a bigger pop at night, just put a bit of golden eyeshadow in the center of the eyelid (two taps with a brush) and draw a thin line only to the outer third of your lid using a brown eyeliner. Finish with some highlighter on the inside corners of your eyes. This technique and color shades are flattering with all skin tones and it is very easy to recreate.

Lips. A tinted balm will do.

If you have extra time: My sister, who is a pro in makeup, told me this trick. If you are applying lipstick, always use a lipstick brush, otherwise it looks too heavy. Then define your lips with a lip pencil (yes, first lipstick, then lip pencil) and finally, use a lip balm to seal the color and blend the lip liner. It looks better and lasts longer!

Product Recommendations

Remember that the most important thing for a "no-makeup" look is radiant skin. Make sure that you clean, moisturize, and wear sunscreen daily. Your skin is the true foundation of this look. The most important part of your makeup routine is your skincare routine. Now, here are my product recommendations for the "no-makeup" look:

Base

* L'Oréal CC Cushion

* Laura Mercier Tinted Moisturizer

* Coola Rosilliance™ Organic BB Cream

* Fenty Beauty by Rihanna Foundation (For a night out. There are 40 shades available. Try the Foundation Shade Finder online or at Sephora.)

Powder

* Clinique Almost Powder

* Laura Mercier Translucent Loose Setting Powder

Concealer

* Mac Concealer N20 (Goes with almost all skin tones. This one is my favorite and it lasts for a long time. I prefer the one with a sponge.)

* Maybelline Fit Me Concealer

* Nars Soft Matte Complete Concealer Light 3 Honey (For your melasma patches. This is a lifesaver if you suffer from this condition. This shade suits almost all skin tones. Or check with someone in Nars or Sephora to find the right shade for you.)

Highlighter

* Mac Mineralize Skinfinish in Soft & Gentle (for lighter skin) or Global Glow (medium and darker skin)

Brows

* Anastasia Beverly Hills Brow Powder Duo color

* Anastasia Beverly Hills Tinted Brow Gel

For both products, go with a shade that matches your natural color or go a shade lighter.

Cheeks

* Make Up For Ever HD Blush. (I prefer cream blush, as you can apply it with your fingers if you are in a rush.)
* Nars Orgasm Blush or Nars Orgasm Liquid Blush (The universal blush shade that goes well with every skin tone.)
* Sephora Collection Blush & Luminizer On the Go Stick
* Sephora Colorful Face Powder in Passionate

Eyes

* **Eyelash curler.** Shu Uemura, Sephora, or MAC
* **Mascara:** Lancome Hypnose, Benefit They're Real, L'Oreal Voluminous Original, Maybelline The Falsies Volum'Express, Maybelline Great Lash.

Eyeshadow

* **Brown eyeshadow:** MAC Saddle Matte
* **Golden eyeshadow:** Artist Shadow Make up Forever.

(Both go well with every skin tone.)

Lips

* **Lip Liner:** NYX Peekaboo Neutral
* Sugar Lip Treatment Fresh in Honey
* Burt's Bees Tinted Lip Balm in Red Dahlia (it can be used as blush in a pinch while on the go)
* Burt's Bees Gloss Lip Crayon in Sedona Sands
* Revlon Colorburst Balm Stain in Honey

Lipstick

* Nude shades: Mac Velvet Teddy Matte, Mac Whirl Dirty Rose Matte, Wet N Wild MegaLast Bare it All, and Rose Bud (This is a drugstore brand that I like. All the lip colors are rich and stay for long time.)

* Red shades: MAC Cosmetics Lipstick Ruby Woo, Wet N Wild MegaLast Lipstick Red Velvet

Even if you don't have time to do the whole thing, make sure that you have a bit of foundation, blush, mascara . . . whatever you feel you need the most. If I'm in a rush, I use blush, concealer, and a bit of lip gloss, and I curl my eyelashes. Remember, you are the mother of a newborn, and you may be busy and tired, but you can look your best with minimal makeup to match the charm of your baby.

When in Doubt, Wear Sunglasses

If there is anything I thought I'd miss as a stay-at-home mom, it was my working wardrobe. I have always loved clothes, and I made a big effort (and spent some big bucks) to look smart and elegant at work. I used to plan all my outfits for the week every Sunday.

This conversation happened a lot when I was leaving for work:

Husband: "Are you going to a fashion show or to work?"
Me: "To work."
Husband: "Don't you think you look too much?"
Me: "I AM too much."

Anyway, after working all my life wearing professional attire, I really had fun putting together my mommy wardrobe. And I don't miss my formal dress at all! When I go out with my baby in the stroller and see young executives walking by in heels, I wonder how they do it. Just a year ago I was one of them, wearing heels from 8 a.m. to 5 p.m. through the week.

Mommy Wardrobe Advice

Don't let yourself get trapped in your maternity clothes for too long. You will get comfortable. I wore the same maternity pieces for so long during my pregnancy that, even though I had to wear loose clothes for the first few months, I wanted something different.

Pieces to have in your wardrobe:

* 1 pair of nice jeans (I like Zara's jeans). If you are still wearing jeans with big pockets and decorations on the butt, please burn them. If you have the budget, J Brand jeans are a great option; look for the ones made with more viscose (usually 43%) than cotton. They look like denim but actually feel like leggings, which makes you move, look, and feel better. They are so thin that they are perfect for summer days when you're not ready for a skirt or shorts, and perfect for when you are flying. They are not cheap, but they will last you forever, and you'll want to wear them every day.

* 2 inexpensive jeans for play dates and park days

* 1 pair of loose casual pants

* 1 pair of denim shorts. Please, classy shorts that don't show a bit of your butt; you are a mom now!

* 1 lightweight jacket (I love military green; it goes with everything and isn't as serious as black.)

* 1 jean shirt

* 5 tops or tight T-shirts, spandex/cotton blend

* 1 black sweater

* 1 colorful sweater

* 1 feminine pastel color blouse that you can wear loose or tucked in

* 2 very loose T-shirts, black and gray

* 2 slinky camisoles (spaghetti-strap, black ones are the best)

* 2 cute nursing tops (You don't need to spend lot of money

on these. I like the Milk Nursingwear and Latchedmama brands. One black and one that is colorful or has a pattern.)

* 1 white blouse (it will blend with the spit-ups)
* 1 blue-and-white striped top (perfect for casual wear)
* 1 long black dress
* 1 nice hat for when you have bad hair days
* 2 colorful scarves (very useful to hide any of baby's spit-up or puking)
* 1 pair of nice sneakers
* 1 pair of flat shoes (I love the brand Soludos; they are very comfy and stylish. Target has great styles, too.)
* 1 pair of decent heeled black boots (to wear on date nights or parties with friends, not with your baby)

What Do I Wear When...
First month: Meeting friends for coffee so they can meet the baby

Maternity jeans. (I know, still!)

Cute nursing top (you will feel more confident if you have to nurse). Please do not buy the spaghetti straps with a clip. They look cheap, are translucent, and they do not make your cleavage look nice. If you like them, wear them underneath a jean top or only at home. Flat shoes.

Month 5–6: Night out with friends; I still wear loose clothes...but look at my adorable baby!

Avoid prints, vibrant colors, or too many colors. Wear black or neutral tones like gray and dark blue. If you want to wear a dress with prints, use a long black jacket. For winter weather choose a straight coat, not button-up. Don't button up your blouse, and preferably, choose three-quarter sleeves or up to the top of the elbow. Stick to V-neck, which brings attention to your beautiful face. Try a V-neck wrap dress for extra slimming power. Wrap dresses are perfect and comfortable for the summer, just remember to choose dark colors. For skirts, pencil looks great. Also, consider wearing shapewear garments under your clothing to slim your figure, smooth out lines, and give you better posture. Use long, thin collars, nothing too tight on the neck; if you wear a scarf, tie it long and loose. Avoid statement belts or very wide belts. Do not wear tight long boots; try ankle boots. Style your hair loose and sleek to make you look younger and more put together.

Play Date

Inexpensive jeans, black slinky camisole or colorful sweater or black V-neck top with a scarf. Sneakers or flat shoes.

Denim shorts with a long-sleeved light blouse and espadrilles. Shorts look more put-together with long-sleeved tops and closed-toed shoes.

Meeting friends for a picnic-barbecue; getting there with my weight loss

Cute jeans, nautical striped top, sneakers.

When in Doubt (and in a hurry)

You can never go wrong with a long black dress.

Spring/Autumn. Long black dress, short jacket, scarf, and black ankle boots.

Warm weather. Long black dress, long soft scarf that covers part of your belly, and flat sandals. You can also add a jean vest.

Even if you have not lost the weight, make an effort to look good. This will encourage you to keep going. And don't fall into the trap of using over−sized dark cardigans. Look for something that gives you shape and don't wear it every day. Other options are a jean blouse (one size bigger only!)

or a green military jacket. Now that we are talking about clothes that keep you warm, please do not wear puffy vests. I mean, seriously, are you cold or are you warm? There is nothing that says "boring stay-at-home mom" more than a puffy vest. Just wear an oversized cute sweater or a fine long jacket and if you are very cold, a scarf or a proper jacket. But please, no puffy vests!

Get rid of your schlumpy things that don't look good on you, so that you're not tempted to wear them (if you have doubts, do a "wardrobe detox" with a friend or family member . . . a cool one, please). Do not entirely forget about your work wardrobe; some of your dresses and pants (the comfy ones!) will look good with flat shoes or even sneakers and you will look more stylish! Remember your posture; stand up straight. Your stomach will look flatter, and you will look taller and more confident. It will even give you an energy boost. Finally, I know you love how easy they are to wear, but please, no workout clothes after midday. Go ahead, put your baby in the bouncer and prepare for the day. Honor yourself! You'll feel better.

Where to Get Fashion Updates and Buy Clothes

Just because we are moms does not mean that we cannot wear the latest fashion trends. As fashion in general is moving toward a more casual look (sneakers, flat shoes, jeans, sporty look . . . even PJs!), take advantage and discover new trends to recreate your wardrobe. There are only two rules, which I did not always apply before my baby: it has to be comfortable and it can't need ironing.

Website

There are so many fashion websites but I cannot waste too much time looking at them. I have been following The Zoe Report by stylist and designer Rachel Zoe (I love her!) and her team, since it was launched in 2009. Its fashion section includes street style, style tips, celebrity style, must-have pieces for the season, and fashion trends. They also tell you the best buys from retail stores such as Zara, Target, and Forever 21. They do the research for you, and then you just buy it online.

Cool Instagram Moms

Do not follow too many "yummy mummys" on Instagram (more about social media in chapter 4). Their perfect outfits (including the baby's outfit, of course!), stunning locations, and cute baby poses (that you can never seem to get with your baby) will drive you insane. Anyway, you know that social media is not real, right? These are my favorite fashionista Instagram moms that give me inspiration:

@Somethingnavy: She lives in New York. Great outfits, amazing shoes, perfect hair. You want to hate her, but she and her daughters are adorable together. She mostly wears luxury brands but her outfits can give you an idea of what it is in fashion at the moment.

@TheFashionbugblog: This is a very "posh mum" who lives in London. She is effortlessly stylish (European after all!). Some of her outfits are from High Street clothing brands such as Topshop and Zara. Just get what she buys!

@Hellofashionblog: Her style is comfy and casual yet trendy. She is always going to fascinating destinations. I want to do my hair up like hers but have yet to succeed.

@SincerelyJules: She is not a mom . . . yet. She is a California girl, globetrotter that dresses very cool and we want/need to be cool, like her!

Copy Cat!

It's great to take inspiration from Pinterest or Instagram, but also very time-consuming. You can still get inspiration on the go at the shopping center, a restaurant, even the playground, when you see a look that you like. I had a mommy playdate once and the other woman was wearing black capri pants, white sneakers, and a loose white blouse, and she had her hair pulled back. I really liked her look and realized I had all the pieces for the same outfit, but I had never put them together! (Of course, I never wore it when I was with her!) Look at the mannequins at your favorite stores. When I don't have that much time to shop and look at every single piece of clothing hanging, I try to get what the mannequin has in my size (it's usually the best option in the store and they have it already matched). I try it at home and if I don't like it or it doesn't fit me, I return it.

Retail Shops

Zara. 85% of my wardrobe is from Zara. They have two big sales during the year: summer (end of June) and on Black Friday. Go to the store a couple of days before and try on everything that you like. Enjoy your turkey on Thanksgiving Day and—at midnight East Coast time—ready, set, go . . . online of course! The kids' line is adorable, too.

Target. Well, I am a mom, so of course I shop at Target. I especially like buying their swimsuits, cover-ups, and shoes, as well as almost all of the boy collection for my son!

Old Navy. Yes, the favorite sport brand of every woman is LuluLemon. I have a couple of pieces and the quality and designs are great. I like Nike, too. However, I am very impressed with Old Navy's sports line. The materials and trendy designs will fit your body and budget! I also like Forever 21 sports bras.

A'gaci. This is a new discovery. It is a very affordable clothing store that you can find at malls and online. If you dig in, you can get the latest seasonal finds at a very reasonable price. The shoes are great too; I have seen very cute flat sandals for $10!

I have Lost All the Weight and I Want to Show Off

Good for you! Just one word: tight. I was so happy when I finally lost all my baby weight. It was close to Halloween. I had never worn sexy costumes for Halloween, even though that is the American tradition. The year before, I was a superhero with my 4-month baby belly. (This was how we told our friends we were having a baby.) We hosted a party and introduced ourselves as The Incredibles and the Incredible Baby. For the next Halloween, after the baby was born, I wanted to wear the tightest leather suit I could find. I bought a pair of cat ears and put on some makeup and viola! I was a cat! When I was posing for photos with friends and doing my cat pose, a friend asked why I was acting like a cat when I was a bunny. I said, "No, I'm a cat." My friend pointed out my large, pointy ears. They were in fact, bunny ears! I had been so excited about my leather suit that I hadn't paid attention to the ears. Cat, bunny ... I did not care! I just wanted to wear something tight. From that moment, I started to transition from my loose clothes to tighter clothes. It felt good. Skinny jeans, short sweaters, and cute vests. I was proud and feeling like my old self again. Meow!

Accessories
Hat

Hats will be your savior for bad hair days (e.g., I-have-not-shampooed-in-a-week hair, frizzy hair, washed-but-not-blown-dry hair, hair with a mask treatment, and of course, the ever popular I-don't-care-hair.) You should have one for every season:

Summer. Brim hats. A big brim is best for sunny days when you are planning to be outside for a long time. A hat with a smaller brim is good to wear with a cute outfit.

Spring and Fall. Floppy fall hats (my favorites).

Winter. Knit beanie. What is better than covering your head and finishing with a big fluffy ball?

I like the hats from World Market, Urban Outfitters, Forever 21, Aldo, and Nordstrom (teenager section; they are cheaper).

Warning. Baseball caps are only allowed when you are in your workout clothes and, of course, at baseball games!

Bag

Apart from your diaper bag, you will need a smaller bag for your personal belongings, such as a cross-body bag where you can keep your phone, car keys, cash and cards. This is a time-saver from having to dig around for your phone, wallet, and keys everywhere in your diaper bag, stroller, and car. In addition, it's safer. There will be moments when you will leave your stroller parked somewhere. The smaller the bag, the better. A medium bag is not practical when you have your baby in a carrier or when you are chasing around your walking baby. I like the brand Bandolier; they have practical and stylish hands-free crossbody iPhone holders with slots to hold your cards.

Jewelry

This is a good chance to get rid of jewelry that you no longer wear or that is out of style. As a new mom, just keep it simple. I like one tiny necklace with your baby's initial. An initial is nicer and more subtle than the whole name. There are necklaces from $50 to $2,000 with diamonds. My favorite brands that have the initial pendant necklace are:

* Jennifer Zeuner

* Monica Vinader (Available at Nordstrom)

* Roberto Coin (Available at Nordstrom)

* Jennifer Meyer (if you can afford it!)

Subscribe to their newsletters. You will receive 10– 20 percent off when you subscribe and they will let you know when they have special sales.

and . . .

* A nice pair of fake diamond studs (or real!!) or pearls
* A watch (I prefer big, chunky masculine watches.)
* Your wedding ring (It feels good to be able to wear it again!)
* Sunglasses (I am not a fan of sunglasses with the big logo or designer name on the temple. My favorites are the classic Ray Ban, though they aren't very practical when you're a mom; you can't put them over your head. Another favorite brand of mine is Illesteva, they aren't super expensive, and their Leonard style seems to suit most faces.)

And of course, when you are not feeling your best or when in doubt, just keep your sunglasses on . . . even in Starbucks.

Beauty Sleep is Not a Myth

Sleep is the best meditation

—THE DALAI LAMA

Lastly, but the most essential ingredient in your daily beauty routine is sleep! I wasn't aware of the importance of good sleep until I became a mom. Before my baby, I used to say proudly that my body didn't need much sleep. Even on weekends, I was up by 7 a.m. (Now I want to slap the old me; I should have been sleeping until noon!) When I heard people say that their best beauty secret was sleep, I thought it was a lie. But in order to have amazing skin, you need to sleep. But more important, in order to enjoy and look after your baby, you need sleep. The first months are hard with the crying and feedings every two hours. I know the first months are difficult; you just survive. And the popular phrase "sleeping like a baby" suddenly has a completely different meaning. (Clearly, they are not describing YOUR baby!) After your baby goes to sleep at night, it's tempting to stay up late cleaning the house, watching TV, paying bills, talking on the phone, or just browsing the internet. If you are sleep deprived, you are not alone. According to the latest Gallup poll, 42 percent of all American adults get less than the recommended amount of sleep (seven hours). Quality sleep is important for your health, your mind, your brain, your beauty, and your baby. How can you take care of your baby if you feel tired all the time? Your number one priority is to look after yourself so you can look after everyone else. A well-rested parent (as much as possible) is just as important as a well-rested baby. Sleep deprivation can lead to depression, marital stress, child neglect, and dangerous accidents.

In her book *The Sleep Revolution*, Arianna Huffington notes the most important recent finding is that sleep is essentially like bringing in the overnight cleaning crew to clear out the toxic waste proteins that accumulate between brain cells during the day. Basically, if you value your brain, get more sleep.

Furthermore, Huffington mentions how lack of sleep has a major impact on our ability to regulate our weight. In a study by the Mayo Clinic, sleep-restricted subjects gained more weight than their well-rested counter-parts over the course of a week, consuming an average of 559 extra calories a day. People who get only six hours of sleep per night are 23 percent more likely to be overweight. Get less than four hours of sleep per night and the increased likelihood of being overweight climbs to a staggering 73 percent. This is largely due to the fact that people who get more sleep produce less of a hormone called ghrelin, the "hunger hormone" that increases your appetite.

Yes, I Know Sleep is Important But...

You must be thinking, "Thank you so much for reminding how important sleep is and how negatively it impacts my body and baby if I don't get it, but I think you are forgetting that I have a tiny human at home and am hardly getting any sleep." OK, here's what you do:

First, make a date with your bed and stick to it. Set the alarm for bedtime. You cannot control how long you are going to sleep when you have a baby. The only control we do have is bedtime, at least after month two or three (even if you'll be waking up in the next few hours for feeding).

When you finally have a routine with your baby, try to go to bed early. I put my baby to sleep between 7 and 7:30 (I hope that you are putting your baby to sleep between 7 and 8 p.m.) and I go to bed at 10:30. There were a couple of months that I was feeling tired and cranky and I made two commitments to myself: go to bed at 10:30 and leave my phone in the living room. In the first months before doing this, I'd feed my baby at 10:30 and then stay up on my phone—checking my baby apps, clothes, Amazon, news and gossip sites (more gossip than news) or looking at all my baby photos videos from the day. I was going to bed at 12:30, sometimes 1:00 a.m.! The recommendation is to stay away from your phone for at least one hour before bed but try for at least 30 minutes of screen-free time before hitting the sack. It really works. Studies have shown that artificial light from screens can inhibit melatonin production, which plays a huge role in telling your body that it's time to sleep. Once I was trying to get my baby to sleep, and I was on my own and very tired. To distract him, I let him play with my phone . . . (I didn't do it often; don't judge me!) I showed him videos of himself and we did FaceTime with my mom—he ended up going to bed at 8:30. It was the only time he'd gone to bed this late and I'm sure the late screen time was the reason.

Bedtime Routine

The idea is to build relaxation into your evening routine. Experts advise parents to establish a routine for their babies, but adults need this, too. It lets our bodies know that bedtime will be here soon. I start my routine at 10 p.m. and leave my phone in the living room. A 2015 nationwide survey of 1,000 people found that 71 percent of respondents sleep with or next to their smartphones. Are you part of this percentage? I take ten minutes to pick up the mess around my house (only ten minutes, otherwise I can stay up until midnight cleaning), then I take a quick shower with the lights off (use candles or a nightlight), finish my tea, apply my face creams (paired with burning a lavender candle is extra soothing), and I go to bed. I try not to think about things that I have pending or that are bothering me. I try to think about the best moments of the day with my baby, then I just focus on my breathing—which is a form of meditation. I am so relaxed and tired that I go to dreamland straight away. It has had a big impact on my mood, energy levels and even my skin. I didn't have uninterrupted sleep for almost the first year but I was able to get at six or seven hours in, largely due to this routine.

Insomia

I doubt you'll have this problem, but there might be days that you just cannot sleep, or when you wake up to soothe your crying baby in the middle of the night and then you can't get back to sleep. Instead of looking at your phone and reading all the horrible things that can go wrong with your baby (yes, I am guilty of this), what about working on your skin-care routine? If you missed any of the nighttime steps, you can use this time to catch up, or even give yourself a nice hand or foot massage. Then go to bed again and try to meditate. When I am having a hard time getting to sleep, I listen to one of the free meditations on the Calm app and in less than five minutes, I am gone. Another recommendation is to use progressive muscle relaxation, individually tightening and releasing muscles from your feet up to your shoulders and neck, after lying down.

Having a healthy diet, spending time outdoors in natural light, and doing some sort of energy-burning activity like cardio, swimming, yoga, or a stretching exercise can help you relax and fall asleep quicker and sleep better.

Natural Sleep Remedies

Melatonin, often used for the treatment of insomnia, is found in more natural substances than you might expect. According to agricultural research studies, cherries are one of the only natural food sources of melatonin. The recommendation is to have some an hour before bedtime. I buy frozen cherries from Costco and usually have a handful at night. Also, you can raise your melatonin levels with pineapple juice, orange juice, a handful of walnuts or almonds, or a half of a banana—which are rich in magnesium, a muscle relaxant. A teaspoon of honey can help too, as honey contains glucose, which tells your brain to shut off orexin, a chemical that triggers alertness. Lavender sheet spray can also help you feel more relaxed.

And remember, do not drink coffee in the evening (six hours before you go to bed) and avoid hard cheeses, spicy, and fatty foods.

Sleep Training

This is not supposed to be a baby book, but since your sleepless nights are frequently due to your baby not sleeping through the night, let's talk about your little rascal. I read all the books about sleep training. I even had a sleep training consultant come to my home, which cost $200! (But hey, that's cheaper than a divorce. *wink*) The biggest regret of my baby's first year? That $200. What was I thinking? Actually, I wasn't thinking at all; I was sleep deprived. It shows how desperate we were.

I did not agree with Ferberization. You will only know this term if you are a baby-book junkie like me. It sounds like freezing fat from your thighs; wouldn't that be nice? (Actually that is called CoolSculpting, but we are not going to talk about that in this book.) The Ferber method is to let your baby cry. I heard this so many times, but I thought to myself, there is no way that I am going to let my poor little angel cry. One day when my baby was 11 months (yes, 11 months, don't judge me) my British mother-in-law came to visit us. We put him to sleep and he started crying. I was about to go and pick him up as usual, when she said to me in a very firm tone, "Do not go in." If it was my mom, I would have said, "Are you out of your mind? This is my baby and I am not going to let him cry." But coming from her, it felt like Margaret Thatcher giving me an order. I have so much respect for her that I just went back to the sofa and sat down. I had a couple of tears running down my face because my baby was crying non-stop. This went on for 20 minutes. The next day it was 15, the next it was 10. In the end, when I put my baby in his crib, he'd stand up to give me a hug and then lie down again and roll to one side. I'd leave the room and see him with his eyes still open, very calm. I could not believe it. My husband was upset that we didn't do it sooner, but I felt that I could not have done it when he was smaller. After my mother-in-law left, we moved him to his own room (again, don't judge me) and he started sleeping through the night at 11 months, 1 week and 3 days. I even took a selfie the next day and sent it to my mom and sister: *This is how you look after eight hours of uninterrupted sleep. Cheers, Granny!*

You Don't Need a Book, You Need a Chapter

For everything related to sleep issues or sleep training, I recommend the book, *Bringing Up Bebé—One American Mother Discovers the Wisdom of French Parenting*. Pamela Druckerman offers studies and interviews about how French babies sleep through the night by three or four months old, or even sooner. Just go straight to Chapter 3, "Doing Her Nights." I read several books on this nerve-wracking subject and this chapter is much better than any of them. To summarize, do "the pause" when the baby is a few weeks old: pause a bit when he cries at night, before picking him up, the mother should pause to make sure he's awake. Between midnight and five A.M, parents should re-swaddle, pat, rediaper, or walk the baby around, but the mother should offer the breast only if the baby continues crying after that. If after month four, he is still waking up, it will break your heart but let him cry it out either by going cold turkey or in stages. At the end it is a very personal choice but the case studies, interviews with experts, and the research that the author presents will give you some insight to help you make your decision. It works in France and it worked for me!

Please, Go to Sleep

Just as your body needs nutritious food and exercise to function properly, it also needs rest. Sleep gives your body and brain a restoration period it needs to, process, repair and restore. When you're sleeping, your brain starts to process your memories from the previous day and primes your memory for the next one. Your energy and your mood also depend on the hormones your body releases with deep sleep. And beauty sleep is real. Your skin cells regenerate and repair the damage caused by free radicals during the day. So if you want, great skin, less stress and a stronger immune system, you need to get your sleep. Only if you are rested will you feel strong and able to focus the next morning. You don't have to feel guilty or stressed about it; sometimes the most productive thing you can do for your sanity and health is to sleep.

Part Four
Hello World, what did I miss?

You have been enjoying your baby at home and recovering from labor. Finally, you feel ready to face the world, to shower and dress up more, put on some makeup, and catch up with friends. And why not make new mommy friends too!

This is not only the time to be a mom, but also to reinvent yourself. You have this amazing opportunity to stay home and be with your baby, and even though this will take a lot of your time, you will also have time to improve yourself: Read books, exercise, cook healthier food, be in contact with your friends more often, and perhaps meditate (OK, at least for five minutes?). Whether you are going to be at home for six months or a year or two, it doesn't have to be 100 percent focused on your baby. Remember, the most important thing is your well-being: if you are well, so is the baby. Taking care of yourself is key for the proper development of your baby.

In this next section, I'll share some tips for taking the world by storm.

Find Your Tribe

I thought that I was going to find my soulmate. The perfect new friend with a lot in common. We were going to breastfeed at the same time, walk with our strollers by the beach, and drink coffee while our babies had uninterrupted two-hour naps. Unfortunately, none of this happened. Most sadly, the two-hour uninterrupted naps never happened.

In order to make new friends, you have to make an effort. There are so many baby groups. Before I had a baby, I didn't think I needed them. Now, they are a blessing. They helped keep me and my baby sane (especially me). You and other new moms are going through the same things and everyone is eager for advice, to talk and to make new friends. Here are some of the classes that I took:

Note: For exercise classes, always consult with your doctor first.

Baby and Me Yoga Class. This is a perfect class to start with because the baby is not moving around. He will be next to you, staring at you and getting to know a different but quiet environment. You will be able to relax (if your angel doesn't cry!), stretch, and talk with moms after the class.

Stroller Strides. This is part of Fit4Mom, which is the country's largest fitness tribe with mama in mind. Stroller Strides is a stroller-based fitness program designed for moms with little ones. Each 60-minute, total body workout incorporates power walking, strength, toning, songs, and activities. They recommend waiting until your baby is at least 6 weeks old. This a good class to start with but requires more energy. The baby will likely be napping through all your movements with the stroller, so you'll be able to exercise. It will be intense, but if you want to get back into shape, this is the course for you. Losing weight while you make new friends! The moms meet at their local park. Check online for a location near you at www.fit4mom.com.

Storytelling at Your Local library. When my baby was three months old, my husband used to take the baby for a stroll. I asked him where they had gone, and he said the library. The new San Diego Central Library was two blocks from our house and I had never gone (in my defense, I used to work from 8 to 5). So I started going to the library, too. I quickly found out about the storytelling class once a week and I discovered "my corner": lots of baby books about how to sleep, breastfeed, and have a calm and happy baby. I borrowed them all and read them all at home. Before, I was spending an average of $40 a month at Amazon on baby books that I didn't even read. Libraries are a great place for babies. They will enjoy being indoors if the weather is too hot or cold (in our case, it was a very hot summer) and love all the colors, the quiet, and enjoy seeing different faces. Any kind of subject that you are interested in ... you 'll find it there. Trust me. You and your baby will love the public library. You will be able to meet with moms from the area and the classes are free. Make sure to subscribe to the audiobook service, too.

Sign Language Classes. The only words that he learned were "milk," "stop," and "eat," but these are the most important ones, especially "stop"! It was worth it, but you do have to be persistent. I enjoyed learning the signs for myself, too. It was very interesting and I will always remember these signs.

Gymboree. We started going when my son was ten weeks old and it was the perfect! They really helped me encourage him to do tummy time, and they teach you so many activities that you can do with your baby at home. Because you can attend several times during the week and most of the babies will be around the same age, it is more likely that you will make good friends there.

Breastfeeding Support Group. OK, I did not make any friends there. The only time I went was when my baby had a bit of reflux when he was about three to four months old. I was fully recovered, dressed decently (remember the mommy dress code), and I was a pro on breastfeeding. I only went because I had questions. Everybody gave me the "don't even try to talk to me" look, and I understand. I would have been the same in the early, tired, and anxious days. They all had their huge and sore breasts out, and their babies were so tiny that it was hard to believe they were real. My baby was the biggest every time I went. So personally, it did not work for me as a place to meet new mommies, but they were amazing for giving advice not only on breastfeeding, but also on sleeping and they were very sweet to my baby.

Your Local Museum. You can become a member of your local kids' museum. I did it when my son was about seven months old and it was great. Go during the week for a greater chance to meet local people. It is a good place to have mommy dates. You can catch up with friends in a safe environment where your kids will be able to crawl around, unlike at a coffee shop or restaurant where you will have to keep a constant eye on them. When your baby is too active, go to the museum!

Local Parks. I didn't start going to the parks in my area until my baby was nine months old and crawling all over the place. I wish I had gone earlier. It is, according to my personal research, the best place to make friends. I think I made a new friend every time that I went, or I at least had very interesting conversations. (In this case, "interesting" means things

145

like "how did you get your baby sleep through the night?") By the time we started going to the park, I was more relaxed about being a mom, my baby was already crawling, and I was more confident about starting conversations with other moms.

YMCA. I did not personally use this option, as I am a member of a gym very close to my house, but I have friends who go there and they love it, especially because they have a free daycare while you are at the gym. Zumba class with other moms while they look after your baby? Sounds amazing!

Be Persistent. Don't be discouraged from trying another group if you find yourself in one that's not a good fit. Making new friends is not going to happen overnight. Be persistent; you might go for the first month and feel like you didn't click with anyone. I would come home frustrated and say to my husband, "No one is my target market." I kept going to different classes, trying to learn more about the moms to find similarities. I remember asking the moms: Are you going back to work? I didn't want to make an effort with the working moms because I knew I wouldn't hear from them after maternity leave. I kept going to classes, with not much hope. Then one day I went to my morning exercise "mommy and me" class that I hadn't gone to for a while. I decided to stay after class so my baby could play with the other babies, and I started talking to one mom. She asked if I spoke Spanish (my first language), our babies were almost the same age, and we lived in the same neighborhood. She had a very charming and easygoing personality and I thought to myself . . . *finally, this is my girl!* I had found my first proper mommy friend. I had been going to the same gym for six years and had not made even one friend. I was always focused on exercising and going home. But at the mommy classes, I was open and friendly and, if I liked one mom, I would ask for her number or tell her my plans for the week and ask if they wanted to join us. Sometimes I felt like a dude trying to find a new girlfriend in the city. It was worth it though. My social circle expanded, and these women gave me tips and told me about new places they'd discovered to go with their babies, and my baby had more playdates!

Don't Forget Your Old Friends

I have lived in Colombia and London, and I have friends in San Diego who now live in other cities, so I have friends in different parts of the world and different time zones. I used this time as a chance to also reconnect with them. With apps such as WhatsApp and FaceTime, there is no excuse not to. Besides, you could be the trending topic in your social circle! Everyone wants to know how you're doing and how cute the baby is. This won't last long, so take this as an opportunity to catch up with friends, especially during the third and fourth month when you've established more of a routine and the baby is taking longer naps or several short naps during the day (hopefully!). I became closer to some friends that I hadn't been in touch with for a while, due to my work schedule and time zone differences. It was nice to share stories of my new life as a mom and hear about how they were doing. Having said that, if you want to disappear from the world for a couple of months, it's your decision. Just remember that having friends and positive relationships is good for your overall health. Quality contact with quality people is what makes a real impact in our lives. University of Michigan researchers who tested 3,610 people between the ages of 24 and 96 found that even 10 minutes of social interaction improved cognitive performance.

The book, *The Danish Way of Parenting* by Jessica Joelle Alexander and Iben Dissing Sandahl, mentions that, "when a woman gives birth in Denmark a local midwife gets her details and contacts her within the first week to check if she and the baby are OK. She also gives the new mother names and contact details of all the other women in the neighborhood who have just had babies, too. These women form groups and meet up once a week to share their experiences and provide support. This helps both mothers and babies feel happy and secure." And they know a thing or two about happiness as they have been voted as having the happiest people in the world by the Organization for Economic Cooperation and Development almost every year since 1973.

It's a stereotype that stay-at-home moms are lonely for a reason: you can easily feel isolated unless you make an effort to prevent it. When we become moms, we become a bit pickier about who we want to spend our free time with. You should definitely surround yourself with people who value you and are important to you. In fact, Dr. David Spiegel, the head of the Psychiatry Department at Stanford, said, "One of the best things a woman could do for her health is to nurture her relationships with her girlfriends." He also said that research has proven that creating and maintaining quality personal relationships with other humans is good for our physical health. Just make a commitment with your friends. Liking their photos on Facebook isn't enough!

Mommy Code

When new moms get together, there is an expectation that certain topics are off limits, do not mention your birth story or, even worse, ask a new mommy friend, "Did you have a natural birth or C-section?" If she did not have a good birth experience, she won't talk to you next time. This is a very sensitive topic. I was actually surprised that no one in my mommy groups asked me. In Colombia, that is the first question you get.

Other questions to avoid: "Are you breastfeeding? How long are you planning to breastfeed?" What if your new friend couldn't breastfeed and feels bad about it?

Never say things such as, "My baby is advanced. He is so smart," or "He is three months and already wearing six-month-old clothes. He is so big!" to the mom with a tiny baby. Don't ask questions and then follow up with your great experience. *Your baby is not eating well? Mine eats everything, she is such an adventurous eater! Your baby is not sleeping through the night yet? Mine is already sleeping twelve hours. I woke up today at 9 a.m.; we are so blessed.* People sometimes brag about their positive experiences to feel better about themselves. Do not fall into this trap. Of course, you can mention your positive experiences to your new mommy friends, just be mindful and sensitive of others.

Never be unkind or ignore texts or calls from other moms. I had a couple of moms who ignored my texts for playdates. Even though it didn't bother me, we kept running into each other and I could tell that they felt quite awkward when they saw me. You will be doing the same activities and going to the same places; the chances of seeing them again are very high! It does not mean that you have to say yes to every invitation, but be nice and gracious with all of the moms that you meet and always reply to a text, even if it's to politely decline an invitation. And of course, don't feel bad about "rejection." Not everyone has to like you, just as you don't like everyone.

Don't be part of the working mom versus stay-at-home mom controversy. Who is happier? Who is more fulfilled? Life changes day by day and we cannot even be sure of the situation we will be in next year. Let's support each other, exchange experiences, and share enriching moments with each other and with our babies.

If your friend's baby has a scratch, a bump, or a bad haircut (all of this happened to my poor angel), don't question it with your worried face. Even worse, don't ask your friend's wounded baby with your baby voice: "Oh no! What happened to you, little guy?" Chill. He is fine, thank you for your concern, we are taking care of it. This is what you'll want to say to this kind of question, but just ignore it.

And, finally, if you see a mom, friend or stranger, with a cool outfit, glowing skin, or looking great overall, let her know (only if you mean it). You will make her day!

Your Time is Precious— Organize It

I t's very easy to say "I don't have time" as a new mom. But is this true or just an excuse? What about when your baby has a nap, when you get help from your family or friends, or when you put your baby to bed? Be mindful of your time. It is very easy these days to fall into the social media trap and instant online access. It's very tempting when you have a minute for yourself to slump on the couch and check your phone. The next thing you know, your baby is awake, and you didn't accomplish anything. (Ask me how I know.) Everyone is given the same number of hours in a day. It's how we use them that differ.

Brian Tracy writes in his book *No Excuses*: "Time management is a core discipline that largely determines the quality of your life. Time management is really life management, management of yourself rather than time or circumstances."

Even if we're not working, we need to manage our time; actually, *because* we are not working, we should be more mindful of our time. It's very important to organize our days, weeks, and weekends, and even our free time.

For the first months, it is difficult to plan your days, as your baby sets your schedule. But from month four or five, when your feeding, sleep, and play routine is more settled and you start going to mommy and me classes, making mommy friends, and getting back to your exercise routine, you should always plan ahead. What works for me is visualizing what is next. On Sundays, I start thinking of which baby classes I am going to in the upcoming week, and I find an open space in my schedule to have a playdate with a mommy friend. Thursday, I go grocery shopping so that I don't have to run errands on weekends. Then I look at the remaining time and see which days I can exercise or see a friend at night.

In his book *The Productivity Project*, Chris Bailey writes that the best technique he has found for working deliberately and with intention every day is the Rule of 3. At the beginning of each day, decide which three things you want to accomplish by the end of the day. Do the same at the start of each week. It could be simple things such as making a doctor's appointment, something tedious like doing the laundry, or a more demanding task such as finishing a book or going to a spin class. At the end of the day or the week, you will be happy that you accomplished it. He also points out that the Internet can destroy your productivity if you're not careful. Just disconnect from it. You don't need to answer every single text immediately, like a post on Facebook, or check Instagram every 30 minutes. Switch your smartphone to airplane mode. Chris Bailey values his productivity too much to stay connected all the time and so should you.

Take a "Moment"

If you feel too hooked to your phone, download the free app Moment, which tracks exactly how much time you spend zoned out in front of the phone. (You will be surprised how much time you spend. I was!). It even gives you a breakdown of what exactly you did on your phone and sends a daily notification about how long you spent on it the day before, compared to two days ago. Remember, there is a big team behind every app who works to get you hooked and keep your attention for as long as possible. Sounds a bit scary, doesn't it? Download this app, and if you are going to check something online, check that and nothing else. Then enjoy your baby, enjoy your surroundings, enjoy your life.

Plan Your Weekends

Apart from planning your week, it's a good idea to plan your weekends, too. I usually go with my husband for a drink on Fridays (for him!) in the early afternoon, and we plan our weekend. When we get home, we write our schedule for the weekend down to the hour on a board on our fridge. Some couples use the Google calendar, but the fridge board is good for us. If you have plans on your own, this is a great time to let him know that you need help with the baby and not to make plans on that day. As you plan your weekends together, your excitement grows about your plans together. Also, when you write things down, you are making a real commitment and are more likely to do it. This is the kind of conversation that we have on a Saturday morning:

8:45 a.m.: (Me in my pj's, lying on the couch, checking my phone.)
Husband: "The board says that you were going to the gym at 9 a.m. and coming back at 10 for me to go after, so go!"
8:46 a.m.: (Me getting ready to go to the gym.)

Free Time

As a new mom, I'm sure you're laughing at this term, but believe it or not, you will have free time. It's very important that you make a commitment to rest and find time for yourself within your new crazy life. As you plan your days with your baby, plan your free time, too. I try to make the bed and clean here and there while the baby is awake, so I don't end up cleaning the entire time he naps. Then, while I am playing with my baby, I start deciding what to do during his upcoming nap time; do I want to exercise, read a book, have a nap? Once my baby is down for his nap, I waste no time and go directly for what I was planning to do. I take my book out, get my exercise mat ready, or start getting the ingredients together for a nice recipe. Whatever you want to use your free time for, plan it, and do it straight away. Don't waste time.

Brigid Schulte, author of the book, *Overwhelmed: How to work, love, and play when no one has the time,*" mentions research that shows when people have a sense of choice and control over what they do with their free time, they are more likely to get into flow, that engrossing and timeless state that some call peak human experience. Part of the problem with leisure is that people aren't quite sure what they really want from their leisure time, and they never slow down long enough to figure it out. Just think about what you really want to do and write it down. What do you want to experience during your time off? Be honest with yourself and think about what would make you incredibly happy.

Time for Exercise

A week has 168 hours. If you work out one hour per day, six days a week—which most moms find doable—you can use only six hours of the week on your body. I prefer to work out at night, since during the day, I am more focused on my baby, his food, and my messy house. If I have free time during the day, I like to use that time to eat, read, and clean up a bit or have a quick nap.

Invest time in yourself and your body will change. Don't think of exercise as a chore but rather as a reward. Being active helps you burn calories, improve sleep, and feel better about yourself overall. It's a gift to yourself.

I try to plan my days ahead, and always try to squeeze in some kind of exercise. If I know I won't have time to go to the gym that night, I go for a longer stroller outing in the morning, go to the Stroller Strides class, or I just do a couple of yoga poses at the end of the day to stretch. If there are days that I really don't have the time or energy, I tell myself it's OK, tomorrow is a new day.

You need to always be connected to your body, just like you were when you were pregnant and you knew that you needed to rest, stretch, sleep, or to eat more. Try to listen to what your body needs. Your body is always talking to you. Some days it's more beneficial to have an early night and catch up on sleep than to exercise.

Build habits that are good for your well-being in the long term. Exercise is one of them. Commit to it. If you say, "I don't have time," you are saying that you don't have time to feel better about yourself. Use your time well.

Use Your Phone as Your Personal Assistant

Before my baby, I never forgot anything: friends' birthdays, doctor's appointments, things to do. I never needed to write most things down. Now, I rely on my phone for everything, from my grocery list, questions for my pediatrician, to ideas for this book. As soon as I make an appointment, arrange to see a friend or receive an invitation, it is on my phone immediately. I also set an alert to remind me the day before. Set up alarms for all your friend's birthdays (at least the closest). You might forget a couple of them this year, and you have the best excuse, but your friends will appreciate that you haven't forgotten about them.

Baby Routine

This is not a baby book. I am not a pediatrician or a baby expert. But I feel it is important for you and your baby to have a routine, so I'll tell you what worked for me. There are a couple of books that helped me establish a routine. One I recommend is *The New Contented Little Baby Book: The Secret to Calm and Confident Parenting* by Gina Ford. She gives different routines for the first year according to your baby's age. Because of this book, my son takes a two-and-a-half-hour uninterrupted nap in the afternoon (he was 12 to 13 months when this happened), and let me tell you, your baby's naps are key to being a happy stay-at-home mom. (The day this ends I am going to die!)

Our schedule at 9 months:

7 a.m. Wake up; diaper change

7:15 Nurse

7:30 Playtime while I make breakfast for him and a smoothie for me

8:00 Breakfast for baby

8:15 Clean baby; more playtime

9:30 Baby nap time. I have breakfast while I watch the news, get ready, and cook lunch for him (if I did not prepare something the day before)

10:15 Diaper change, baby class, library, park, or a walk in the stroller

11:45 Lunch for baby and nurse

12:30–2:30 Baby naps. Thank you, Dear Lord!!!

Me: Check phone, eat, make phone calls, do the dishes, do stretching exercises, or read a book

2:30 Nurse, then outdoor activity

4:00 Baby snack

4:15–5:30 Playtime with Dad while I cook dinner and rest a bit or go to a gym class. (Yes, I know. I am very lucky that my husband's starts work early and is back home early.)

6:00 Baby's dinner

6:30 Give baby a bath, nurse, and prepare baby for bed (Please!)

7:15 Breathe, remember my name, check my phone

7:30 Dinner with husband, do dishes (sometimes together)

8:00 Work out if I didn't earlier and I have the energy; otherwise, watch TV with husband

9–10 Work on this book

10 Quick shower, beauty routine, pick up mess around house

10:30 Meditate in bed, sleep

Remember, your baby is not the only one who needs to be on a schedule every day. You should have one, too, and keep it.

Shape Your Husband Like a Rough Diamond

"Do the dirty work. A human being will exit your wife, so she has done enough. Just change the diapers."

—RYAN REYNOLDS ON WHAT ADVICE HE WOULD GIVE TO DADS
POST-BIRTH. (AS IF WE DIDN'T LOVE HIM ENOUGH!)

My husband and I met in London at a nightclub. I know, it sounds tacky. I wish I had met him at a museum or a library, about to pick up the same book. He spoke to me in Spanish with the strongest Argentinian accent, asking me if I spoke Spanish. I said, "Yes! And you are from Argentina, right?" "No," he said, "I am English." I said, "No, you are not! You are from Argentina." He insisted that he was English so I asked him to speak to me in English and as soon as he said "pardon," a very English word, with a Hugh Grant accent, I said, "OK, you are English." It turned out that he had lived in Buenos Aires for eight years. We have been together since. After years of living in London, he got an offer to work in San Diego. San Diego? The only place that I had been in the U.S. before was Miami. I went straight to Google images, and the first photos that I see are the perfect and sunny beaches. After seven years of cold windy winters and summer temperatures that averaged 69 degrees, I said, "I am sold! Let's go." He reminded me that I wouldn't have any friends or a job there, but I didn't care. Just take me to the beach. I knew I would love to live in a sunny place. And that is how we ended up in the United States.

My husband was very attentive during my pregnancy and after the delivery. If your husband is not very helpful with your newborn (or in other words, useless), you can make it work.

Your husband is like a diamond in the rough, and you have to sharpen it to find the sparkle. You can't tell your husband to just help with the house or go grocery shopping. You have to be very specific about what you need, such as, "Could you please take the garbage out, clean the sink, and change the diaper pail? I will text you the food list. Thank you!" When you give them specific tasks, they can accomplish them more easily. From the beginning, ask them to change diapers, dress the baby, and help you with bath time. If they can't do these things, you'll be damned. You won't be able to go out with friends until after bath time or leave your baby for any length of time if he doesn't know how to change a diaper—your baby would be in the same diaper for six hours. And unless you see your husband suffocating your baby with a blanket, do not point out when he does something wrong. Don't discourage your husband from helping. If you are reluctant to hand over responsibilities or you criticize your husband's efforts, he'll do even less. Give him confidence. Every time he does something well, say, "Good job, Daddy! You are doing an amazing job," the same words that you would like to hear once in a while. Even if your mom, your sister, or a nanny is helping you, do not spare your husband from the baby chores. This will help him bond with the baby, and he will be a big help when you are tired, need a nap, or are going out with friends. You will know that he can be in charge. I absolutely trust my husband. He is even better at getting our baby to sleep than I am. You also have to be considerate of each other. Take turns. You go to the gym while I look after the baby, and when you come back I will have a nap. We did the same thing when we had our first vacation. I would stay at the garden with the baby while he read a book by the beach. After we had lunch together during the baby's nap, it would be my turn to be by the beach and he would play with the baby.

Being equal partners in raising your baby and sharing the housework has no downside. Yes, he should help with housework; just because you stay at home doesn't mean you do not need help. We need it and deserve it. Research has even shown that when men and women share the housework, they have more sex!

In addition, Sheryl Sandberg tells us in her book *Lean In* that studies that children benefit greatly from paternal involvement. Research shows that in comparison to children with less involved fathers, children with more involved dads have better well-being and cognitive abilities, higher levels of educational and economic achievement, and are more empathetic and socially competent.

Find ways to reconnect with your husband. Check in with each other emotionally and keep the lines of communication open. Be considerate to one another, and don't forget special occasions: birthdays, Father's and Mother's Day, and anniversaries. Base your relationship on respect, admiration, and compassion. It's hard to be a good wife when you're so focused on being a good mother, but you must make an effort to have a healthy relationship. Touch base with each other on a daily basis. That is why it's so important that your baby has an early night schedule. Babies need regular bedtimes for their own health and to give parents a break and an opportunity to work on being a couple. You need regular time together without the baby; those couple of hours at night are precious (even though you will sometimes wisely use them to get extra sleep).

Have a small ritual every day. I have a friend who bathes with her husband every night. (Um, OK, they don't have any kids yet!) In our case, we have dinner together and watch TV after we put the baby to bed. We don't check our phones while we are eating and only watch TV shows that we both like. And when you are ready (usually it takes longer if you are nursing), reconnect with yourself as a woman, with your own sensuality. Buy a new fragrance, new lingerie, or a red lipstick for a night out, and plan something different and fun with your partner.

There are going to be challenges, strong emotions, and stress. They are all a natural part of becoming parents. But at the end of the day, it is worth the effort. The authors of *And Baby Makes Three*, John M. Gottman and Julie Gottman, put it very well: The greatest gift you can give to your baby is a happy and strong relationship between the two of you.

Keep Up With The World

had a friend who came to see me when my baby was a few months old. She gave me the great news that she was pregnant. I was so excited for her and also to know that my son was going to have a new friend. We talked about all the things that you have to do in the first trimester—and that was just the pregnancy stuff.

It occurred to me to mention all the celebrities that were pregnant around that time. I mentioned about ten! My friend was surprised that I knew so many names, and not in a good way. I felt embarrassed and mentioned that I had too much free time on my hands. She said, "Yes, I burned some brain cells, too, when I was living abroad with my husband, and not working." She didn't mean it in a bad way, but it made me think... Was I at risk of losing significant brain function because I wasn't working anymore? In my defense, this was when my baby was three months old and I was just kind of waking up to the idea of being a mom. Also, what else do you do when you are nursing every two to three hours, 20 minutes each boob? (Ehh, Daily Mail anyone?) As I said before, you can let it go for the first weeks or months, but then you have to catch up and keep up with the world. Just because you are a stay-at-home mom does not mean that you are rejected from society. Never stop growing intellectually. Feed your brain every day.

Watch or Read the News. There are so many apps and newsletters with the headlining news of the day. My favorites are the *New York Times*, *Buzzfeed News*, and, my super favorite, *theSkimm*. This is a daily newsletter that gives you everything you need to start your day. They do the reading for you and break down the latest news and information with a friendly and easy-to-understand tone. Even when my baby is still waking up in his crib, I can have a quick scan of this newsletter. Also, when I am in line at Starbucks or waiting for my coffee, I try to scan the first page of the *New York Times*. It gives you a glance of the most important news for the day and tons of conversation starter points, besides your new bundle of joy. Did you know that today was the hottest day in history in India? 120 degrees Fahrenheit. Wow!

Good Morning America! I love GMA. I remember being late for work the day that Diane Sawyer left. When I was working, I used to get ready while watching the news. I don't like watching TV with my baby so I record it and watch it during his morning nap or while I breastfeed. This way I can watch the news and skip commercials.

Keeping up with current events allows you to talk to your friends about things other than your experiences as a mom, the weird rash that came two days ago, and his constipation. For this kind of conversation, pick a very close friend or even better, a relative. Also, be careful about saying things like "This is the happiest that I ever been." It's fine to share your joy, but don't tell them every time, especially to your childless friends; some of them are not childless by choice.

Whether you get information from the radio, TV, websites, or from a quick scan of your local newspaper, it is important to know what is happening around the world, and I am not talking about who Leonardo DiCaprio's new girlfriend is. This will not only provide you with conversation topics, but will expose you to information that will help you or affects you directly, like baby product recalls, latest research on infants, baby hazards, health concerns, and recent studies about babies and toddlers. I personally benefited from all that information. Having said that, you don't need to know every single thing that happens in the world. You don't need to read every single news alert or every detail of the news that is interesting to you. You have enough worries and little time. Also, there is a high chance that you will be more sensitive to sad or bad news. Be selective of the media that you choose and the time you spend on it.

Art and Culture. Appreciate how others observe the world. Visit museums. (This is fun to do while your baby is napping in the stroller.) Go to the theater (try to look for independent films) and listen to music, really paying attention to the lyrics. Read biographies of people you admire or other books on whatever subject you are interested in. Reading a book can be a great distraction and will keep your intellect awake; when you finish a book you feel accomplished. I love reading and I had to read a lot for this book. My goal was to read three books and listen to one audiobook every month. One book per month is a doable goal.

I really enjoyed going with my son to the zoo, the children's museum, and parks, and taking him to the beach, but I also needed to "feed" myself. Try to do something cultural at least once a month with your husband, a family member, or friends.

You are teaching your baby so many new things every day; take some time to teach yourself something, too! Make a plan to figure out how you can find time to explore your interests.

Don't Overshare on Social Media

"With Twitter, Facebook, and WhatsApp, who has time to chill out? Life has become a constant search for outside stimulation with no road map inward."

—GABRIELLE BERNSTEIN, *ADD MORE -ING TO YOUR LIFE*

I'm sorry if this sounds harsh, but you are not the only woman in the world who just had a baby and the only ones who think that your baby is the cutest in the world are you and your closest family. They are the only ones who want to receive updates on your baby on a daily basis and even they don't want photos of your baby's poop! It is a very personal choice, but I wonder how I would feel if there were thousands of photos of me as a child on the Web. According to one survey, parents will post almost 1,000 photos of their children online before the child turns 5! Consider what could happen to our babies when they are older; everyone will know their story. If you still want to share your happiness with the world online, go ahead, but try not to post photos every day or complain or brag about motherhood (those are the worst). "Breastfeeding at 3 a.m. I am so tired!"

Staying off social media saves time and can also save you from the "comparison trap." Even though you have a baby, you could get a bit jealous of your single friend posting photos of her trip to Italy or the party that you missed where all your friends look amazing. Everyone is busy creating a digital life that does not really exist, and it is hard not to compare our lives to everyone else's. And the attraction of social media can reach concerning levels. Not to be dramatic, but you could get distracted to a point that, in the worst case, you neglect your child.

A study from the University of South Wales presented in 2017 reveals that receiving likes on social media posts doesn't make people feel better about themselves or improve their mood if they are down. Also, Tristan Harris, a former Google executive and co-founder of the movement *Time Well Spent* www.humanetech.com, mentioned during his TED talk in April 2017 that the apps on our phones can lead people to feel dissatisfied with their lives.

Something that really works for me is that I don't have the Facebook app on my phone. Every time I want to check Facebook, I have to go to the website and log in. (I would not dare do that with my Amazon app! It even has my fingerprint). That makes it more difficult for me and sometimes I cannot be bothered to do it. It is like when you really want to buy something online and are about to check out only to see that they don't have PayPal. (How do websites or companies not have PayPal? This is beyond me!) You are too lazy to look for your card and you forget about the purchase. This way, I don't check my Facebook account every day or, even worse, several times during the day. Remember, as the American writer Annie Dillard says, "The way you live your days is the way you live your life." Do you want to live your life on Facebook? Social media is not real; it is what people want you to see. Do not compare yourself with your friends (or friends of friends). Just do your best and be grateful for what you have. As Mark Twain once said, "Comparison is the death of joy." Social media can be entertaining, but people get way too consumed. I am not suggesting that you quit social media. Just be mindful of the time you spend on it, and please, unless you are posting the first photo of your newborn, never use the hashtag #blessed. It is annoying.

To wrap up this chapter on keeping up with the world, remember: don't gossip.

"Great minds discuss ideas; average minds discuss events; small minds discuss people."

—ELEANOR ROOSEVELT

If You Don't Love It, Leave It!

No, I'm not talking about your husband. I'm talking about decluttering your house. When you heard this word, you might only think about your closet, but what about the rest? To get you started, I highly recommend the bestseller *The Life-Changing Magic of Tidying Up* by Marie Kondo. One of the best tips that I got from this book was, "We should be choosing what we want to keep, not what we want to get rid of. Take each item in one's hand and ask, 'Does this spark joy?' If it does, keep it. If not, dispose of it." I applied this method and let me tell you, I got rid of a lot of unnecessary stuff. Kondo recommends sorting by categories, not location. Start with clothes and end with mementos, and you will be surprised by how much junk you have. And finally, make it a festival, not a chore (which probably doesn't apply to new moms, for whom the only joy is sleep). She recommends discarding and tidying in one shot, as quickly as possible, but for us busy moms, this just isn't realistic. If you're pregnant and feel up for it (and you have a very helpful husband), please follow this advice. I did it with my husband before the baby arrived and we got rid of so much unnecessary stuff. You have to make space for all your baby equipment. According to the National Soap and Detergent Association, getting rid of clutter eliminates 40 percent of housework in an average-sized home.

Try to check for clutter every week, including baby stuff. Lend things that you no longer need to your pregnant friends (you always have one!). If you are planning to have a bigger family, store things away until you need them again. In each closet, have a donation box for any outgrown or unwanted things.

The most important part of this is maintenance. Clean as you go. Make a habit of putting everything back at the end of the day. We don't worry that much about toys, books, or things that our son takes out during the day. We make sure that the kitchen is always clean and that we make our bed and keep our room clean. At baby's bedtime, my husband cleans while I put him to sleep or vice versa. I also spend ten minutes at the end of the night cleaning up and making sure that I have things ready for the next day. The more I do at night, the less I have to do in my crazy mornings. Perhaps it is difficult to have a perfectly clean house with newborns and all the chaos that they bring with them, but at least you will know that you need the stuff that you have. Also, it makes you think twice when you want to buy more stuff.

I also like to have a weekly project, something small: clean up my jewelry drawer or the medicine cabinet (check which medication has expired), get rid of clothes that I don't wear anymore, purge the shoe shelf, organize the grain storage (I recently put all my grains in glass containers and I love it).

"I only do one of these tasks a week, and only when I have extra time, such as when my baby is napping longer than usual or when my baby is already sleeping and my husband is out for the night. Also, ask your husband to be responsible for his own belongings. You have enough picking up to do after your baby.

Organize your home in ways that will make your daily life easier. If possible, splurge on your sanity by paying for some help from a housekeeping service, once a month, twice a month, or weekly. I have a housekeeper once a week and she is a blessing. If possible, commit her to a certain day during the week, so you don't have to think about it anymore. Besides her regular chores, give her a specific project every time that she comes. Choose something that you cannot be bothered to do: clean the windows, the oven, a wall. If you think you can't afford it . . . are you sure? Give up Starbucks, cancel your cable TV, dress your baby only from Carter's on sale, remortgage your house. Ok, I am only kidding, but please find a way, at least once a month. Otherwise, make sure that you divide that housework between you and your husband, especially the first months.

The Only Way to Organize Paper Clutter

Get rid of it. You only need essential papers such as tax returns, mortgage documents, car titles, one file for your baby with all your stuff. Sign up for paperless billing and pay online. If you are pregnant and reading this, just do it now.

You do not need to keep paper instructions of anything; you can find them online, or even better, YouTube will show you how to use your baby k'tan. Register your address at DMachoice.org to stop junk mail by category (credit cards, catalogs, etc.) or individual merchant. Junk mail should go directly to the garbage, and discard newspapers and catalogs after reading them. About 80 percent of what we file away never gets looked at again, according to the National Association of Professional Organizers. Also, look for unread books, magazines, and stuff that belonged to someone else. Give it back!

A Clean Car is a Happy ... Mom

In addition to your house, you should clean your car on a regular basis. You and your baby spend a lot of time there. Do not overload it with clutter and trash. Wash it regularly (ask your lovely husband to take it to the car wash) and take all the clutter out whenever you can. According to my own research, 96 percent of the time you will be carrying your car seat with your baby sleeping, and you won't have the chance to take anything else with you. But whenever you drive alone or go back to your car after putting your baby down, take the opportunity to clean it out. Don't make your car your second home. Only keep a change of clothes, diapers, wipes, sunblock (if your baby is older than six months), and one bag for trash in the car. I have a small one that I put in the center console. Please do not use the floorboards for trash disposal.

Use your baby wipes to regularly clean the hard surfaces and remove dust and dirt (think about your baby's tiny lungs). Your baby wipes are as effective as car wipes, minus the chemicals. I keep a package next to my baby car seat and one in my glove compartment. I like doing this when I am pumping gas. I also empty my car trash bag and any trash that I see. Make this a habit.

Meditation And Mindfulness

"Because it feels good. Kinda like when you have to shut your computer down, just sometimes when it goes crazy, you just shut it down and when you turn it on, it's OK again. That's what meditation is for me."

—ELLEN DEGENERES, WHEN ASKED ON THE *TODAY SHOW* WHY SHE MEDITATES

It is impossible to ignore all the benefits of meditation. There are so many studies and too much buzz to ignore it. You have to cultivate your mind and have a deep understanding of self.

I started meditation just before I started trying to get pregnant. I was in the middle of a job crisis, and I was getting anxious about whether or not to have a baby. There was a point that I felt I could not breathe between my new job responsibilities and thinking... Can I really have a baby? What if I cannot get pregnant, or if I get pregnant right away? How do I prepare? What am I going to do? A friend of mine had recommended meditation a while ago due to my Virgo "everything has to be perfect" personality. I Googled "meditation San Diego." To my surprise, I found several websites and I reached out to the one closest to my house. I signed up for a month. I went three times a week for a 40-minute session and did 8-minute meditations at night on the days that I couldn't go. Unfortunately, I stopped going after the third week. I didn't even last the month, and then the center moved further away from my work. I would love to tell you that it changed my life completely and that I am a calmer and more focused person who meditates every day, but where meditation is concerned, I am a work in progress. It did help me to be aware of the moment and more connected to my breathing. And I am very aware of its benefits. I just have so much on my mind that I struggle to commit to it at that level—and that is the main purpose of meditation, to declutter your brain—I'm working on it. Neuroscientists at Harvard found that people's gray matter expanded after only eight weeks of meditation, yoga, or just noticing how their bodies felt for as little as 27 minutes a day.

If you think meditation is complicated, don't feel discouraged; even the Dalai Lama confessed at the annual meeting of the Society for Neuroscience in Washington in November 2005 that he finds meditation difficult.

Many people recommend meditating first thing in the morning, but that is impossible for me to do as my baby is my alarm every day at 6 a.m. I prefer to do it at night. As I mentioned in the previous chapter, if I am doing yoga at home, I meditate afterward, or just before I go to sleep. I sit quietly in a comfortable position with my feet on floor, or I lie down on my back. I pay attention to my contact with the floor. This is recommended to force you to engage and be present before you work on your breathing. Cross-legged with my hands on my lap, I relax my face and close my eyes. I focus on my breathing. I breathe deeply three times with my mouth closed and then I imagine a lot of clouds in motion. Every thought I have—what is the weather going to be tomorrow, what do I need on the grocery shopping list, did I take the baby clothes out of the washing machine—I treat as clouds that just come and go, and then I gently bring my attention back to my breathing. I try to focus on my breath coming in and out, and I really focus on when the air is passing through my nose nostrils fossils (Or whatever is clearer to you, chest or abdomen). This type of meditation practice is called mindfulness meditation or vipassana. Beginners should focus on a single object of attention, such as the breath. The idea is to do it for eight minutes, just eight minutes before you go to bed. OK, maybe four before you crash from exhaustion. Just try it. Also, at the beginning of your day, take a couple of minutes (or even a moment before you go and pick up your crying baby) to recite one goal or intention for your life.

You look after your body through exercise and good nutrition; take care of your brain, your mind, and even your spirituality through meditation. This practice will allow you to reset the mind and reorganize your energy. Meditation makes your calmer, happier, and more focused and it doesn't have to be intimidating. You learn to be in the moment and practice patience, which will be useful in the near future with your toddler.

If you feel that it can make a big impact in your life, and you have the time to seriously commit to it, research meditation centers in your area. Yoga studios hold guided meditation, too. If you just want to try it, there are lots of apps that will walk you through meditation. Here are some of my recommendations:

* Buddhify
* Calm (My favorite)
* Headspace (The most popular)
* Insight Timer
* Omvana

I also recommend the guided meditations of Gabrielle Bernstein. You can find them on her website at www.gabbybernstein.com. Her book *The Universe Has Your Back* is life changing. I have the audio and print version and I read/listen to it at least once a month.

What about mindfulness?

If meditation seems like too big of a commitment to you, start with being mindful. It is not easier, but it is a simpler start. Mindfulness can be a form of meditation (mindful meditation, as I mentioned previously) but there is also simple mindfulness. There is no one definition for mindfulness, but overall, it is living in the present moment, giving your full attention to what is happening right now— without judgment—just dispassionately observing your surroundings, sensations, and thoughts. Mindfulness is a way of living, and meditation is the practice that helps us to nurture and cultivate mindfulness. (Do you know how much I had to read to figure this out? I even ended up checking out the Oprah SuperSoul Sunday online, which I highly recommend.)

Mindfulness is a state you can cultivate anywhere, anytime—as you eat breakfast, walk with your stroller, wait in line for your coffee, or work out. It sounds easy but in this world of a multitasking and instant digital access, and especially as new and busy moms (some of us anxious), absolute attention to one thing at a time can be asking a lot. How many times are you in the middle of the most amazing yoga class and instead of focusing on your breathing or your movements, you are thinking . . . *How long does this class last? I really need to buy more workout clothes, when could I go? I need a pedicure, too . . . and order more baby wipes!* Mindfulness is that deeper connection to the present. It means being really present with your baby, even when you are changing a diaper (there are many moms who would give anything to change one more diaper). No checking your phone every five minutes. Stay in the present moment in everything you do in your daily life. Pay more attention. Take in everything that is happening around you as fully as you can, and remember, no judgment.

As Bhante Gunaratana explains in his book *Mindfulness in Plain English,* "You cultivate mindfulness by constantly reminding yourself in a gentle way to maintain your awareness of whatever is happening right now. Mindfulness is cultivated by constantly pulling yourself back to a state of awareness, gently, gently." The benefit, according to the author, is that "mindfulness gives us time, time gives us choices. We don't have to be swept by our feelings. We can respond with wisdom rather than delusion." Wow! I really need to be more mindful!

Don't get me wrong: being mindful is a challenge, more challenging than sitting down and with our eyes closed for ten minutes. But at the same time, how rewarding would it be to build the invaluable capacity to really live in the moment, find peace in our crazy-busy days, and not let our emotions get the best of us. That is mindfulness ladies, and therefore, happiness.

Book Recommendation

"Mindfulness in Plain English" by Bhante Gunaratana. It is one of the best-selling mindfulness books of all time. This is a great book, especially for beginners. Very simple to understand and the advice is easy to practice.

If All Else Fails, Just Breathe...

In mindfulness, breathing is an awareness exercise. When you are stressed, your breathing changes and less oxygen enters your bloodstream. The breath is a vehicle for returning to the self.

Try alternate nostril breathing, also known as Nadi Shodhana (which means clearing the channels of circulation). According to Rebecca Pacheco, yoga instructor and author of *Do Your Om Thing: Bending Yoga Tradition to Fit Your Modern Life*, this kind of breathing makes people feel more awake. "It's almost like a cup of coffee," Pacheco said in an interview. This breathing technique settles the mind, body, and emotions. It will bring you back to your center. It is so powerful that Hillary Clinton turned to this practice to heal from her devastating presidential election loss. (I mean, if it helped her, it could help you!)

Take a deep breath and exhale through your nose. Then inhale through your left nostril, covering your right nostril with your right thumb. Cover your left nostril with your left thumb to exhale through your right nostril. Pause. Keep the right nostril open, inhale slowly, then close it with the thumb. Pause. Exhale slowly through the left. This is one cycle. Repeat three to five times.

The Yoga Way

Before my pregnancy, I must confess that I was not a yoga fan. I used to believe that yoga was boring. My favorite ways to stay active were weight training and running. At that time, I was really into long runs and I had completed four half marathons and one Olympic-style triathlon.

But something happened when I started yoga classes during my pregnancy. At first, I found it was a great way to stretch and relax, and I really enjoyed those last five minutes of meditation that allowed me to connect with my baby. Later, after I had my son, I felt that cardio was still too hardcore for me so I kept going to yoga; and finally, I just fell in love!

Yoga is so much more than almost-perfect bodies holding fancy poses on top of a mat. It is a state of connection that has the purpose of calming our minds. It's like a gate that takes you to a peaceful, mindful present. But just like any other discipline, it won't make you feel magically happy and complete the day after your first class. But I can assure you that if you get into it, you will become more present, peaceful, and mindful.

As the mother of a newborn, yoga can help you to self-nourish, get back in touch with yourself, and discover who you are in this new reality. And you probably already know this, but if you take care of yourself, you can be sure that you will be ready to take care of your baby, and to do it more compassionately.

On the other side, there is an immediate relief after yoga. You can feel it in your arms and back muscles, which deserve a great stretch after holding and feeding a newborn baby, and in your legs, which will gain strength and ease your balance. And if you had a baby through vaginal birth, yoga can help you re-engage with your pelvic area, and that may improve your sex drive, something that you and your partner will enjoy. Namaste to that! Plus, as I evolve in my yoga practice, from my beginner days holding a belly until today, yoga taught me that motherhood comes with no guidelines, with both happiness and bitter moments, patience and mistakes.

In motherhood, you need to be ready to face your days in many different ways, but yoga will be there to help you return to your center. And that's priceless, especially once your newborn turns into an energetic toddler!

So, where to start? If you haven't tried it before, or tried it and weren't into it, please try it at least three times during one week to decide if it's really for you. If you are a gym member, almost all gyms have yoga classes. You can also join a yoga studio. If you simply can't leave home, just buy a yoga mat and go on YouTube to learn some poses. All you really need to practice yoga is your mind, body, and spirit.

The next step will be to find what kind of yoga suits you best. All of them can improve your strength, flexibility, and balance. Hatha, restorative, and yin yoga are great for beginners and vinyasa is better for more advanced practitioners. Here is a brief description of some of the types of yoga that are available to you:

Hatha

Generally, a class marketed as hatha will be a gentle introduction to the most basic yoga postures. You probably won't work up a sweat in a hatha yoga class, but you should leave class feeling longer, looser, and more relaxed.

Yin Yoga

Look for this if you want to stretch while you calm and balance your body and mind—in other words, find your Zen. Yin yoga poses are held for several minutes at a time and can help you restore length and elasticity.

Restorative

This is a slow-moving practice with longer holds that gives your body a chance for a deeper relaxation. While supporting your body with props, like blankets, bolsters, and yoga blocks, it can help you repair your muscles, ease your mind, relax your bones, and nurture your spirit.

Vinyasa and Ashtanga

Maybe because I am very active and I really like feeling like I worked out, vinyasa is my favorite yoga. Vinyasa classes have movement-intensive poses and sequences that are linked to the breath and transition smoothly. The intensity is similar to Ashtanga, but no two vinyasa classes are the same. In contrast, Ashtanga always has the exact same poses in the exact same order. Both are hot, sweaty, and physically demanding practices.

Bikram and Hot Yoga

Neither Bikram nor hot yoga are my personal favorites, but both will make you sweat buckets! I consider Bikram classes too long and boring. All Bikram classes follow the same series of 26 poses for 90 minutes inside of a heated room. Hot yoga is also in a heated room but the sequence is slightly different. Because the classes are so long and physically challenging, I would not recommend them for a new mother. However, I started practicing hot yoga seven months after having my baby and that definitely helped me sweat out some extra pounds and got me back into shape.

Now that you know what kind of yoga suits you best, you can settle your own routine and adapt it to your goals or to your mood on a given day.

If you really want to practice yoga but money and time are tight, you can try these popular YouTube channels; all you need is a mat, a good Wi-Fi connection, and an adventurous spirit.

* Tara Stile's yoga practices are intense and quick; she will help you gain strength with straight-to-the-point videos that last 3 to 15 minutes.

* Yoga by Candace has simple and calming sequences that are narrated with a soothing voice. She will invite you to relax and enjoy her routines, which last from 15 to 30 minutes. Candace also has her own website with longer classes and a blog with yoga and fitness tips.

* Yoga with Adriene feels designed for beginners because she has very casual, easy, and even ways to guide you through her routines.

My Favorite Yoga Poses

Downward Dog

Warrior II

Triangle Pose

Best Poses for Sore Backs

Cat and Cow Pose

Child's Pose   **Happy Baby Pose**
(balance side to side)

Even if you don't have much time to exercise or if you feel tired and stiff after a long day of taking care of your baby, take time for yourself while your baby is sleeping and practice yoga. If you can, go to a private room and do a couple of poses and then meditate with low music for five to eight minutes.

Finally, remember not to be self-conscious when you practice yoga. It is not about performance, it's about the practice. The good thing about yoga is that there is no judgment, no competition, no comparison. Both yoga and meditation bring greater self-awareness. And never forget: if you can breathe, you can do yoga.

Join a Group

And I don't mean another baby group! If you are not working, consider joining an association or support group related to something that you are passionate about. I was part of the Latina Giving Circle of San Diego, which has the mission of bringing together San Diego Latinas who want to uplift, celebrate, and share the philanthropic traditions and values of the Latino community. I joined this nonprofit when I was still working as a way of networking and making new contacts for my job, and to support my community. I became more involved six or seven months after I had my baby. I became a member of the leadership group, went to their monthly meetings (sometimes with my baby), and volunteered to be the organizer of monthly coffee group meetings. It is great to feel part of a community, gain knowledge, enter a new social scene, and find new mommy friends. It will also help you make connections if you want to go back to the corporate world. You will have a chance to discuss things other than baby topics and, most important, you will have fun!

Reconnect with Nature and Take Your City by Storm

"Look deep into nature, and then you will understand everything better."

—ALBERT EINSTEIN

After I had my baby, I craved contact with nature and really enjoyed going to open spaces surrounded by nature. I was lucky to live in San Diego for the first year of my baby's life and to have the opportunity to do outdoor activities with him year-round. Even though I had lived in San Diego—the most biodiverse county in the U.S.—for six years before he was born, I had been working all the time. This was my opportunity to get to know the parks, playgrounds, and family-friendly beaches of my community. I felt so happy for my baby that he could chase ducks and squirrels in a park, play with the sand at the beach, and be exposed to such amazing landscapes.

Be aware of your surroundings, of the air that you are breathing, the sound of the water. Talk to your baby about everything that he is seeing. Go to the park, sit down by a tree, feed him, get him down for his nap, and focus on the natural world around you. Be in the moment. Try to meditate for three to five minutes or just breathe deeply. It will recharge you.

I love finding new open spaces to take my son. We go to the incredible

Balboa Park at least once a week. But San Diego isn't the only city with great outdoor spaces; take advantage of the city where you live. You will be surprised to discover so many places that are good for your baby that you haven't noticed before. It doesn't matter if you've lived in the same city all your life or you just moved.

In one of my mommy groups, I met a cool mommy from New York. She had just arrived to San Diego in the winter (where the average temperature is 65 degrees), and she was complaining to me that there were not that many things to do with kids in San Diego. I couldn't believe it! I told her I could not imagine what you would do with kids in New York during the winter. She excitedly mentioned several activities to me, which shows that you just need to explore and take the place where you live by storm— museums (not just kids museums), parks, the zoo, libraries, aquariums, playgrounds, kid-friendly restaurants, art galleries, farmers markets, kids shows, and public swimming pools—, even when you think that your baby is too young to enjoy stuff. I have a friend, a mother of twins, who used to take her 5-month-old daughters to the children's museum. She would sit with a blanket in a part of the museum that had soft musical instruments for kids to play. Her daughters enjoyed hearing new sounds, looking at bright colors, doing tummy time, and looking at other children. It is OK if you do not want to do that much the first few months, but at some point, you need to get out. It is good for the baby and it is good for you!

Take Your Vitamin N

In his book "Vitamin N," Richard Louv writes that pediatric professionals are prescribing or recommending nature time for their patients and says research indicates that experiences in the natural world boost the immune system and serve as a buffer to depression and anxiety. The main health benefit is that it gets us off the couch and moving, and he makes his point saying: sitting is the new smoking and the solution is some green exercise.

Make Memories

Once a day, once a week, or at least a couple of days per month, make sure that new-mom memories are recorded so you can look back at them later. One very dear friend came to see me when my baby was only two weeks old, and she gave me a little blue book, a journal for the next five years. I loved that gift and now I try to give one to my friends who have just had a baby, too. Some days I am too tired to write or I forget. There were two whole months that I did not write much, and I regretted it. Even though I have photos of almost every single day with my baby it is nice to know what was going through my mind that day or what cute little thing he did, or to have the exact date of a big milestone.

There are lots of ways to record your memories of your baby. Here are some of my favorites:

Shutterfly. I made an album about my pregnancy and my baby's first year. It is very easy to make, and the quality of the photos is amazing, even using photos from your phone. I also made an album of the baby for my parents as a Christmas present. Keep an eye on offers and special promotions. I usually wait until I find a 50 percent off coupon.

Keep your albums simple. Use white backgrounds and do not include every cute picture of your baby. I usually do a page for every month, and two or three spreads for vacation places, special occasions, or professional photo shoots. I do not add symbols, stickers, or phrases, which take more time than I have. When I make an album, I typically spend two hours doing the layout and uploading the photos and another hour choosing the photos. I work on it for 15 to 30 minutes per day until it's done.

Lifecake. Like Facebook, but just for your closest family and friends, to share only your child's photos and videos.

Photo of the Month. I just put my baby in a white onesie with a sticker on his chest that says how old he is and place him over his nursery rag. I try to take the photo at the same spot every month, with all my blinds open and in the morning to get the same light. I like the simple white outfit because I can see the changes in his lovely chunky legs and for the consistency of every photo. You can get the stickers from Amazon or Etsy. There are also blocks and blankets with milestone numbers on them. At every "month day," I recorded a video of him where I mentioned recent milestones, what he loves or does not like at the moment, or cute and funny things that he has done.

Professional Photos. I had one three days after my baby was born and one when he was seven months old and able to hold his head up. For his first birthday party, I gave my professional-quality camera (that I never use) to some of our closest friends (the ones I knew had talent!) and asked them to take nice photos of us.

Do not forget to back up your files. I lost the photos of my baby from month 8 to 11 when I spilled water on the phone. (Nope, not the baby, it was me!) When I went to the Genius Bar (not so genius, because they could not retrieve my photos!) the guy told me of a woman who had paid $2,500 to get her photos back. She had lost all her baby's photos from birth to six months. (I think I would have paid that, too.) Luckily, I had sent all the photos to my family, and my dad had them all in the cloud. (How could my dad use the cloud and not me?))

Make Time To Play

Shonda Rhimes, the mastermind behind some of TV's biggest shows (*Grey's Anatomy*, *Scandal*, and *How to Get Away with Murder*), revealed in a TED talk that she got her passion back with the help of her kids. She had her dream job but somehow her spark had disappeared, and she could not restart the engine. One day her younger daughter asked her, "Momma, want to play?" She decided to stop working and just play with her kids, and she says that learning to say yes to play saved her life and her career. Pausing to play with her kids recharged her batteries and brought her passion back. Rhimes is absolutely right; play is good for us. It relieves stress, boosts creativity, improves brain function, improves our relationships, and keeps us feeling young and energetic. "Work less, play more" is what experts are suggesting. We are talking now about play deficit in the same way that we talk about sleep deprivation; it is bad for you. As stay-at-home moms, it is very easy to go and play with your baby, but it is also important to play on your own! Just be spontaneous, relax, and be open to new mini-adventures. Play matters, no matter how old you are. There is a reason that arts and crafts classes are so popular nowadays and that coloring books for adults are becoming best-sellers. Researchers at Johns Hopkins University even suggest coloring as an alternative to meditation. It is time to embrace your inner child and go play!

Explore with Your baby

Look for places you have never been before. Discover new things with your baby. Go for a walk that you've never taken, try a new baby class (usually the first class is free), or if you have the financial means become a member of the zoo or museum. Have a picnic date with your baby—bring food and a blanket, toys, and a book or magazine for you for when he naps. At home, put on some music and dance with your baby (they will love seeing you dance). I personally loved going to the playground. I enjoyed going down the slide with my son or swinging next to him. I had not done that in a long, long time. I pretended that I was doing it just to join him, but I was actually enjoying myself! Let loose and feel like a little kid again; you have the best excuse! And remember that a family who plays together gets very close. Sometimes I see tired parents at the playground with a cup of coffee, telling their toddler where they can and cannot go. I am guilty of this too! As they grow older, you don't have to be that close all the time, but as your baby starts walking (between 10 and 15 months), try to be more involved. Don't just be close to them, but play with them, too. Run *with* them, not behind them. Play peek-a-boo or airplane in the middle of the park—who cares who sees you! Be more like your baby, who doesn't care if he looks ridiculous and doesn't worry about whether you are judging them. Have fun with your baby. Play creates joy, and it is also how your child develops crucial skills for future happiness.

Playdates of Your Own

Play is not just essential for your baby. Find ways to "play" or go on "play-dates" on your own. Before I had my baby, I invited a mommy friend, whose babies were 10 months and 2 years old, to a painting class. When we finished the class, she told me half-ashamed, half-excited, that this was the first time that she had done something without her kids. It was a bit shocking for me. I made a promise to myself that I was still going to have fun after having kids, and I have kept my promise. I have not forgotten about myself. I don't go clubbing with friends until 3 a.m., but I make sure that I have time for myself and that I do fun things with my friends. The first time that I left my baby with a nanny for a few hours, I went paddle boarding with my friend for two hours. It was great. I was catching up with her, exercising, being in contact with nature, and doing something fun and challenging. (At one point, I realized I was without a cell phone and started panicking about how the nanny was going to contact me in case of an emergency. Let's just say that I paddled very fast on my way back.) Another time, a very dear friend of mine decided to celebrate her birthday with a twerking dance class and asked me to join her. I said, "Why not?" It was super fun, though my husband wasn't very impressed by the routine when I showed him. But it inspired me to take the dancing class at the gym that I always wanted to take but was too shy to do before.

Think outside the box. It is good for your brain! I accepted any fun invitation from my girlfriends and new mommy friends. (It's very easy to say "no" because of the baby.) A 2016 joint study by the University of Sussex and the London School of Economics shows that relaxing and resting are not the best ways to be happy; it is better to be active instead. Activities such as exercising or going to the theater are more effective. Make time for the things you enjoy, make a conscious effort to increase your joy, and do things you love. Make time to refresh your soul. Finding time for yourself takes commitment, creativity, and determination, but it is worth it.

Make Time to Rest—No One Else will Do It for You

Also try to have some downtime every day. Being mindful and in silence for at least for 30 minutes literally expands your brain and helps you to restore energy. As mothers, we need solitude. Dr. Meg Meeker, in her book *The 10 Habits of Happy Mothers*, says: "Solitude centers us and brings about a deep peace that cannot be achieved while staying immersed in either the good noise of friends and family or the awful noise of raucous media. We must retreat into quiet aloneness so that we can learn to be the women we were meant to be."

You need to commit to having free time, and you have to understand that this time is very valuable. If you want to read a book, go to a yoga class, or even have a nap, respect this time. Think about what you really want to do and make sure to take time for this. With a baby, you have to plan ahead. If you do not plan your free time, you will be overwhelmed by all the options and, because you are always tired, you will be more likely to end up on your sofa checking your phone. And don't feel guilty about taking free time because your husband is the breadwinner. You are looking after your baby all day. You deserve a break.

Find Your Passion

Who looks outside, dreams; who looks inside, awakes.

—CARL JUNG

Before having my baby, I worked in media sales for twelve years in London and San Diego. To be honest, it was not my real passion, but as a foreigner in both countries with English as my second language, and with the pressure to make a living, the easiest job to find was always sales, even though I have a master's degree in marketing and a bachelor's in journalism. I used to console myself with the thought that I had stayed in my field, at least, by doing media sales. I never envisioned my career or what I wanted to be successful at. I'd had those goals in my home country but once I moved to London (where first I had to learn the language) and then to San Diego (where I arrived in 2008, during the worst recession since the Great Depression, thank you very much!) I just felt lucky that I found a job. I was good at sales. I enjoyed the adrenaline that closing a deal brings and the commissions, but my heart was not in it.

My husband and I had always planned that when we had a family, I would stay at home, at least for a couple of years, especially since we don't have any family living in our city. I was content with our decision until I was twelve weeks pregnant and on a business trip to New York. On my flight there, I read a book that a friend recommended to me a while ago: *Lean In: Women, Work and The Will to Lead* by Sheryl Sandberg, COO of Facebook. I could not have picked a worse book to read. Don't get me wrong, the book is fantastic, very empowering and inspiring, but as a pregnant woman about to leave her job and career, it was a terrible choice. According to *Lean In*, after having a baby, the more satisfied a person is with her position, the less likely she is to leave. "With the best of intentions, they end up in a job that is less fulfilling and less engaging. When they finally have a child, the choice—for those who have one—is between becoming a stay-at-home mother or returning to a less than appealing professional situation." Sandberg could not have explained my situation any better. After reading her book, I landed in cosmopolitan New York to have dinner with the Multicultural Director of Macy's and other top marketing executives and agency directors in a very fancy restaurant. They all talked about how wonderful, challenging, and exciting their jobs were. After dinner, I went back to my hotel and called my husband.

Me: (Crying hysterically—remember, 12 weeks pregnant) "I don't want to quit. I can make it work. I can find someone to look after the baby. I want to get to the top. I want to sit at the table. I want to lean in!!!"

My husband: "Sit at the table? Lean in? What the heck are you talking about?"

We all know how this story ends up. I went back to reality in San Diego. I continued working for five months and, after the baby was born, I did not return. In the end, I was happy and confident with my decision and felt blessed that I had this opportunity to spend so much time with my baby.

I agree with Sandberg on so many topics of her book regarding the benefits to women who don't give up their careers. But after working 8 a.m. to 5 p.m. for twelve years in a profession that did not bring me joy, I needed to find another way of reaching my full potential and perhaps, getting an income. I have always enjoyed reading and, since I didn't have a clue about babies, I read all the books I could find when I was pregnant. I considered all of them very useful, but after having the baby, I could not find books about how to take care of myself. I started reading books on the subjects that I was interested in: weight loss, skin care, time management, motherhood, self-help, spirituality, healthy lifestyle, and cooking, as well as books by celebrity moms. I was fascinated with some of the books that I read and disappointed by others. Suddenly, I had an idea: what if I wrote a book about my experience as a mom, the things that I have learned that no one told me about? It came together so easily. After I had my baby, several friends got pregnant and I was always the one giving advice (sometimes unsolicited; I am sorry!). I have always been a beauty junkie, and I had adopted a very healthy lifestyle living in California. I love reading and, even though I had not written much before, it has always come naturally to me.

I am only telling you this to show you that you can find your real passion too. Think about what you are good at. What would you like to do if you could make it happen? What did you want to be when you were studying? What was the dream job that got lost because you had to take a job to pay the bills and then, as you were growing with the company or industry, you never left? This is a new beginning for you. Even if you are not thinking of working for the next few years, what about studying something? Do you know that you can take courses online? I have friends that have gotten master's degrees from universities in Spain, just logging in from Colombia! If you don't want to go that far, you can still read about the subject that you are passionate about. If you have time for social media or for your weekly TV program, you have time to read, to study, to practice. Make sure to learn something every day or at least every week. Commit to reading, listening to audio programs, and broadening your knowledge base.

You have the time now to think about what you really want to accomplish in your life. What makes you feel the most alive? What brings you joy, engagement, satisfaction? It is about being the best version of yourself. You really have to dig deep to find out what you are passionate about doing.

You can have fun pursuing your real passion and you just might find your next business adventure. How do you see yourself in five years? I know it is difficult to even think about the next hour, but time goes by so fast and next thing you know, you will be waiting for your kids to come home from kindergarten. Think about what you want. Would you like to have more babies? Would you like to go back to work? What kind of job would you like? What kind of business could you start on your own? Or even just what would you like to take as a serious hobby?

If you are an artist, what about working on a few samples and selling them on Etsy or to some friends to start with? Are you famous for your healthy cupcakes? Why don't you start selling them to some local bakeries or to your friends for their parties? If you love organizing events, what about offering to set up events for your friends? Get the certification as a yoga instructor that you always wanted or become a consultant of the field that you were working in before you had your baby. I was once in a mommy group and the question of the day one time was, "What do you wish you had more time to do on your own?" Surprisingly, the majority said shopping! I consider myself quite good with clothes. I didn't share this, but I thought, I could be a personal shopper for these girls. I did not pursue this mini-business idea but it just goes to show that there are always opportunities if you keep your eyes open. How many stay-at-home moms are millionaires because they thought of and *developed* a product that they could not find for their babies?

Please note that I said "thought of and developed." It is not enough to just recognize what your real passion is. Once you recognize it, you have to work for it, practice, and make time for it on a daily basis if you can. When I see these Instagram sensations on makeup, fitness, fashion, I know that they work hard for it. They update their profiles and look for good pictures and ideas every day. (I think I would run out of ideas after two weeks!) If they don't post, tag, get more followers, or bring something new every day, they get lost. I am sure that they are very successful because they are passionate *and disciplined*. And now they are making money from it! If you want to get better at anything, you have to practice, and self-discipline is a must.

Motivational speaker Brian Tracy says in his book *No Excuses* "By practicing self-discipline, you become a new person. You become better, stronger, and more clearly defined. You develop higher levels of self-esteem, self-respect, and personal pride." Reinforcing the idea of self-discipline, Tracy also mentions in his book, that he asked Kop Kopmeyer who is a legend in the field of success and achievement, what is the most important success principle that he has discovered? and Kopmeyer quoted American writer Elbert Hubbard, who in 1900 said: "Self-discipline is the ability to do what you should do, when you should do it, whether you feel like it or not."

The single most important element in developing an expertise is your willingness to practice. I committed to writing an hour a day or 1,000 words per week and that is how this book was born, was I committed? Yes. Did I always reach my goals? No. Sometimes it took me months to write 1,000 words. But even when life got in the way, I was committed to returning to the work when I could. You have to be dedicated and enthusiastic, and discipline is key. Discipline is just knowing how to choose between what you want now and what you want in the future. According to Gretchen Rubin's book *The Happiness Project*, happiness research predicts that making time for a passion and treating it as a real priority instead of an "extra" to be fit in at a free moment will bring a tremendous happiness boost. So what are you waiting for? Think about what you really want to accomplish in life and make time for it. No excuses. Stop wasting time watching TV, browsing online, or checking your phone. You feel more alive when you are learning, creating, or discovering something. This is also an opportunity for personal growth. Life is about pushing yourself and becoming a better person every time. Now you have a baby, and that can be more than a motivation to dream big and achieve your full potential. And the best thing is that since you are doing something that is truly your passion, you will find the time to do it. It is not over for you, the baby is the strength; this is just the beginning.

You might be reading this chapter and thinking, "Sorry, too tired to find my passion. The only thing that I want to find is my coffee in the morning." Look for something that comes to you naturally, something that will test your skill level but not to the point of making you feel overwhelmed, then take action in that direction, day by day, until you find yourself immersed in your bliss. If it scares you a bit, it's OK, just move forward. You don't have to look for your passion. Look inside of you and do what you enjoy and it will find you. It found me!

Soon after I started writing this book, I took Elizabeth Gilbert's latest book, *Big Magic*, to a sunny vacation in Cabo with my family. At that time I had fears and doubts about the book. Is it worth it? Was it going to be just a waste of time? This part really inspired me to keep going. I hope it helps you, too.

> *"I want to live the most vividly decorated temporary life that I can. I don't just mean physically, I mean emotionally, spiritually, intellectually. I don't want to be afraid of bright colors, or new sounds, or big love, or risky decisions, or strange experiences. I am going to spend as much time as I can creating delightful things out of my existence because that's what brings me awake and that's what brings me alive."*

—ELIZABETH GILBERT, *BIG MAGIC*

Final Words

When I was pregnant and getting ready to have my baby, I wanted to control everything. But from the day that he was born, I realized that I can't and that it's best to let go of things, to be engaged with life and do things with my baby and on my own that keep me active and give me a sense of fulfillment.

During the first year of my son's life, I was so many different types of "mom." First, I was Eco Mom with a natural birth plan, placenta pills (yes, I had placenta pills. I didn't tell you before because I didn't want you to judge me early on in the book, which you shouldn't anyway, but I digress . . .) nonstop breastfeeding, and yoga. Then I transitioned to a less-exciting phase, Worried Mom: *Is my baby's percentile OK? Why is my baby not crawling yet?* I would ask other moms in my mommy groups how old their babies were, just to compare them with my baby. *Is he as big, tall, and active?* I would take my homemade zucchini puree when we went out and followed my baby around the playground with hand sanitizer. Finally, I achieved the phase of Chill Mom, just a mellow mom who looks after myself, goes on adventures every day, and rediscovers the world through my child's eyes. We eat chocolate croissants (occasionally), I put on the Disney Channel when he wakes up too early (even if he still isn't interested), and I just put a diaper and some wipes in my handbag (please note, no diaper bag) when we go out. I've never reached the stage of Super Mom, as I never saw myself as one.

Since I can manage my day however I want (apart from choosing what time I wake up), I learned the importance of self-discipline, creating good habits, and being consistent. Remember, successful people have good habits. They help to define who we are. The more consistent you are, the closer you will be to your goals. Bad habits are easy to create but difficult to live with. Good habits take a big effort to create and they are even harder to maintain, but they will give you amazing transformations in your life. It is important for everything, from healthy eating habits to your glowing skin or even making new friends. You cannot expect to show up to one mommy and baby class and find your soulmate. You can't wash your face once in a while and have glowing skin. Make a decision, make it part of your regular everyday activities, make it part of your life. Do a 30-minute workout every day, drink hot water with lemon in the morning, meet with a friend once a week, be on time when you are meeting your friends, read one book per month, do a face and hair mask once a week, drink more water, and eat more nutritious food during the day. When you feel that you are in control of your mind and body, you will feel happier, more confident, and more fulfilled.

Start every day with gratitude. When you are grateful for what you have right now, it starts to put everything in perspective. Appreciate everything. You can go through this first year as a mom like a zombie (you'll hear a lot of moms say that they wish they had enjoyed their baby's first year more, or that they barely remember anything) or you can bring passion to everything that you do, (everything, even household chores.) Be mindful of all the time you have with your baby, find joy in the ordinary moments, and cultivate a spiritual life characterized by optimism, certainty, and happiness.

There are so many things that you can do while your baby naps, sleeps at night, and don't be too proud or afraid to ask for help from family and friends. Do not lose your thirst to learn or create things; there is always something to do. This is an opportunity to become the best version of yourself—happier, healthier and more interesting. You will never be the same person again. You are a mom but that doesn't have to mean sweatpants, dark circles, messy hair, muffin top, and not a clue of what is happening in the world. (Though everyone is allowed to have those days—or weeks—once in a while.) That said, don't pressure yourself to do it all and do it perfectly all the time. Be gentle with yourself; take care of yourself. You need the energy. Do not rely on your baby for complete fulfillment. Yes, your baby is the most important thing in the world, but don't put things off just because you don't have time for yourself. As Michelle Obama once said, "You have to prioritize yourself, otherwise you will start falling lower on your list." Nurture your own interests, your passions, and adult relationships. Enjoy the things that make you feel excited and engaged with life. Never forget who you are. Do things that remind you of who you are outside of your everyday life as a mother; doing so is healthy for your whole family. Your husband and your baby will enjoy being around you more.

Don't get me wrong, The first year as a mom is hard. It tests your limits. But it is an opportunity for your best self to shine through and for you to realize just how strong you are. So be a proud Stay at Home Mom, be grateful, breathe deeply, live healthfully, look stylish, be endlessly curious, follow your bliss, be present, keep it simple, love yourself, dare greatly, and . . . do it all over again. Every single day.

As I finish this book, my baby is 1 year old, 21 pounds, 30 inches, and has six teeth. As for me, I lost all the baby weight and a bit more—due to an exotic combination of breastfeeding for 12 months, chasing my crawling baby at 6 months, walking at 11 months and now running! And finally, he began sleeping through the night a few weeks before his first birthday (thank you!). My stomach is flat and my hair didn't fall out, but I might have a few new eye wrinkles—thanks to 11 months of interrupted sleep. I've gone on date nights and my husband is very glad that I am no longer asking how I could have avoided a C-section. But most important—besides this tiny rascal that changed my life—I feel empowered and completely in charge of my body, my mind, and my time. This first year as a stay-at-home mom gave me the opportunity to look inside myself, find my true passion, be vulnerable, accept my limitations, appreciate nature, be open to new experiences and people, and know that everything does not have to be in perfect balance and according to my plan for me to be happy. Furthermore, I expected to feel the deepest, most unconditional and out of this world love with my baby, but little did I know that this tiny human being was going to love and need me as much as I love and need him.

I am aware that this journey is just starting and that it may get harder, but I am very grateful that I had this year to bond with my baby and reconnect with myself. Toddler years, here we come!

The 12-Month Checklist

Wow. As every mother in the world says, it goes so fast! As the one-year milestone is approaching, this is a mini-list of things you can do to help you slowly become your old self... or even a better version.

* Buy a couple of new bras. (Add a serious push-up bra if you breastfeed!)

* Buy a set of sexy underwear.

* Make a dentist appointment for a cleaning.

* Make an appointment with a dermatologist.

* Get a professional facial. (If you cannot afford it, ask for one for your upcoming birthday! A friend, a group of friends, or a family member will be happy to give this to you.)

* Buy a new fragrance.

* Have a fun night out with your girlfriends. Completely glam up for your night out.

* Have a weekend, day, or night out with your husband. Just the two of you!

When You Stop Breastfeeding:

* Use Retinol. Start twice a week and then every other day.

* For melasma or sun spots, use hydroquinone (stop every six months) or Lythera (always check with your doctor first).

* Use Finulite for cellulite.

If You Need It and Can Afford It

* Sclerotherapy for your spider veins

* Laser for your C-section scar

* Laser hair removal

* Viviscal or Biotin for hair loss (Check with your doctor first.)

Do Not Forget

* Wear sunscreen every day. As your baby becomes more active, you'll be spending a lot of time at playgrounds and walking with your stroller.

* Wear a hat when you are out in the sun. It is also a savior for your bad hair days, which as a mom, is almost daily.

* Make your baby one-year album. (Don't forget to backup all your photos!)

* Make one good new habit a day: drink hot water with lemon, go to bed at 10 p.m., read or exercise, use sunscreen, watch the news in the morning, drink more green tea.

* Start adding weights to your workout.

* Take advantage of your fridge and your time at home to make homemade beauty treatments (honey on your face, eggs on your fine lines, banana for acne, olive oil for your dry ends, aloe vera for sun spots).

* Become a member of the zoo or the kids' museum or whatever is close to you. It will be your savior when you don't know what to do or your toddler is all over the place. Museums are a lifesaver on extra hot or rainy days.

* Babyproof your home if you haven't already.

* Put everything that your growing baby is not using, wearing, or playing with anymore in storage.

* Start thinking about your baby's first birthday party! Don't go crazy and trying to use every cool idea you see on Pinterest!

* And finally, besides enjoying and looking after your little angel . . . find your passion, work at it, and have fun!

Happiness Challenge

You don't think you have postpartum depression, but you feel a bit sad, isolated, and introverted. You are not depressed, but you don't feel 100 percent happy. Happiness is a complex state of mind and it takes some work, but here are some activities that may help you get out of a rut:

* Meditate for ten minutes every day (OK, at least five). The Calm app has a great free seven-day beginner's program.

* Do not complain for a whole day. I know, very hard!

* Try to sleep at least seven hours.

* Watch a funny movie.

* Get a full body massage.

* Cook a meal you love.

* Do ten jumping jacks or dance to one of your favorite songs.

* Play airplane with your baby. It will make you laugh seeing his funny faces.

* Have at least one hour of outdoor activity with your baby (weather permitting).

* Spend less time on social media and remember that

everyone is creating a digital life that likely is not true.

* Call or see a friend who you know will make you laugh.

* Text a friend who you haven't seen in a while and make plans to get together.

* Schedule something fun on your calendar to do on your own, with friends or family ... and do it!

* Write down a list of ten ideas. On any subject.

* Exercise every day for 30 minutes. Walking with your stroller counts as exercise! And don't skip it. According to a study, reducing daily activity leads to increased feelings of anxiety, depression, confusion, and anger.

* Reward yourself at the end of the week for something that you accomplished (meditated every day, finished a book, did not bite your nails).

* Work toward a big goal for ten minutes each day.

* Make your baby helpless with laughter at least once a day.

* Keep a gratitude journal and at the end of the day, jot down three things that brought you happiness during the day.

For more ideas sign up at saragaviria.com to receive them in your inbox.

Acknowledgments

To you, the readers of this book: If I made at least one new mom feel inspired, prettier, happier, healthier, relaxed, or more disciplined, or at least made her laugh once, my job is done.

To all the moms that I misjudged before I had kids. The ones I saw with babies in their strollers without shoes or socks, thinking the baby must be so cold without knowing that the little bugger took them off. To the moms of babies with runny noses, (I used to wonder, *Why doesn't mom just wipe his nose?* without knowing that it starts running again after 40 seconds.) The ones that I gave a fake smile to when they told me they enjoy watching *Plaza Sesamo* with their kids (wondering how they could let their kids watch TV). To the stay-at-home moms with a once-a-week nanny who I judged for taking the time off (*why do they need a nanny? They don't do that much . . .*). The ones I dismissed for serving premade mac and cheese dinner to their kids (it's now my lifesaver on a lazy day and the only thing that I enjoy buying in bulk at Costco besides toilet paper). And to the ones that give the phone to their kids so they can put them in a stroller, eat in a restaurant, or travel on a plane . . . (*What happened to books, people?* I used to think.) To all of you. I am so sorry. You all are my heroes and you are doing an amazing job.

To the incredible women who helped me with this book: Lilia O'Hara, my editor and the one who read my first draft, your kind words encouraged me to move forward with this project; my very patient and perfectionist copy editor Kate Nelson, your dedication and focus is much appreciated; Tania Navarro, my second brain, and the talented Jamie Lee Reardin for her beautiful illustrations and for agreeing to be part of this project.

To Dr. Mitchel Goldman for taking the time to review the skincare chapter and nutritionist **Heidi Parish** for her guidance on the healthy-eating chapter.

My friends: I am deeply grateful for my wonderful friends Ana, Gwendolyn, Juanita, and Sandra H. in San Diego, Shadia in Houston, Paola in Munich, and Tatiana and Luisa in London.

To the San Diego Central Library, where I got most of the books for my research, wrote part of this book, took my son to baby classes, and paid a lot of late fees (I deserved it!), thank you for opening an infinite world of knowledge and awakening my curiosity.

My family: To my sister, my best friend and the biggest cheerleader of this book, for always telling me the truth (always) and for unconditional support; to my brilliant dad, who is responsible for my passion for reading and who insisted that I take the fast reading course when I was younger (that helped!). To my very British husband, thank you for listening to me when I needed it and for *not* listening to me when *that* was what I needed. Thank you for giving me total confidence to pursue the idea of this book and the freedom to enjoy our baby at home.

To my spiritual guru, my dear son, I was so ready to teach you everything about this world and then I realized that you were here to teach me about myself and help me see the world again through your adventurous soul.

And lastly, but not least important, the woman that I kicked out of my delivery room, **my beautiful mom**. I still wonder sometimes what would have happened if I had just listened to you. Since that day, I have done everything that you said and . . . you are always right. Your love, good energy, and tenacity inspire me every day. Te amo, mami.

Book Recommendations

James Altucher, "Choose Yourself: Be Happy, Make Millions, Live the Dream"

Chris Bailey, "The Productivity Project: Accomplishing More by Managing Your Time, Attention, and Energy"

Paula Begoun, Bryan Barron, Desiree Stordahl, "The Best Skin of Your Life Starts Here: Busting Beauty Myths So You Know What To Use And Why"

Gabrielle Bernstein, "Add More 'ing' To Your Life: A Hip Guide to Happiness"

Gabrielle Bernstein, "Miracles Now: 108 Life-Changing Tools for Less Stress, More Flow, and Finding Your True Purpose"

Gabrielle Bernstein, "The Universe Has Your Back: Transform Fear to Faith"

Brené Brown, "Daring Greatly: How the Courage to Be Vulnerable Transforms the Way We Live, Love, Parent, and Lead"

Dr. Trevor Cates, "Clean Skin From Within: The Spa Doctor's 2 Week Program to Glowing, Naturally Youthful Skin"

Charlotte Cho, "The Little Book of Skin Care: Korean Beauty Secrets for Healthy, Glowing Skin"

Luiza DeSouza, "Eat Play Sleep: The Essential Guide to Your Baby's First Three Months"

Cameron Diaz and Sandra Bark, "The Body Book: The Law of Hunger, the Science of Strength, and Other Ways to Love Your Amazing Body

Cameron Diaz and Sandra Bark, "The Longevity Book: The Science of Aging, the Biology of Strength, and the Privilege of Time"

Claire Diaz-Ortiz, "Design Your Day: Be More Productive, Set Better Goals, and Live Life on Purpose"

Roxy Dillon, BSc, MSc, "Bio-Young: Get Younger at a Cellular and Hormonal Level"

Dr. Joe Dispenza, "Breaking The Habit of Being Yourself: How to Lose Your Mind and Create a New One"

Pamela Druckerman, "Bringing Up Bebé: One American Mother Discovers the Wisdom of French Parenting"

Angela Duckworth, "Grit: The Power of Passion and Perseverance"

Charles Duhigg, "Smarter Faster Better: The Secrets of Being Productive in Life and Business"

Dr. Wayne Dyer, "10 Secrets for Success and Inner Peace"

Emily Flake, "Mama Tried: Dispatches from the Seamy Underbelly of Modern Parenting"

Gina Ford, "The New Contented Little Baby Book: The Secret to Calm and Confident Parenting"

Bethenny Frankel and Eve Adamson, "Skinnygirl Solutions: Your Straight-Up Guide to Home, Health, Family, Career"

Elizabeth Gilbert, "Big Magic: Creative Living Beyond Fear"

John M. Gottman, Ph.D., and Julie Schwartz Gottman, Ph.D., "And Baby Makes Three: The Six-Step Plan for Preserving Marital Intimacy and Rekindling Romance After Baby Arrives"

Bhante Gunaratana, "Mindfulness in Plain English"

Dan Harris, "10% Happier: How I Tamed the Voice in My Head, Reduced Stress Without Losing My Edge, and Found Self-Help That Actually Works—A True Story"

Dr. Christina Hibbert, "8 Keys to Mental Health Through Exercise"

Arianna Huffington, "The Sleep Revolution: Transforming your Life, One Night at a Time"

Jill Kargman, "Momzillas"

Gary Keller with Jay Papasan, "The One Thing: The Surprisingly Simple Truth Behind Extraordinary Results"

Mastin Kipp, "Claim Your Power: A 40-Day Journey to Dissolve the Hidden Blocks That Keep You Stuck and Finally Thrive in Your Life's Unique Purpose"

Mastin Kipp, "Daily Love: Growing into Grace"

Katie Kirbi, "Hurrah for Gin: A Book for a Perfectly Imperfect Parents"

Sarah Knight, "Get Your Sh*t Together: How to Stop Worrying about What You Should Do So You Can Finish What You Need to Do and Start Doing What You Want to Do"

Marie Kondo, "The Life-Changing Magic of Tidying Up"

Harold Lancer, "Younger: The Breakthrough Anti-Aging Method for Radiant Skin"

Richard Louv, "Vitamin N: The Essential Guide To a Nature-Rich Life"

John Medina, "Brain Rules for Baby: How To Raise a Smart and Happy Child from Zero to Five"

Meg Meeker, M.D., "The 10 Habits of Happy Mothers: Reclaiming Our Passion, Purpose, and Sanity"

Shauna Niequist, "Present Over Perfect: Leaving Behind Frantic For a Simpler, More Soulful Way of Living"

Rebecca Pacheco, "Do Your OM Thing: Bending Yoga Tradition to Fit Your Modern Life"

Gretchen Rubin, "Better Than Before: Mastering the Habits of Our Everyday Lives"

Gretchen Rubin, "Happier at Home: Kiss More, Jump More, Abandon Self-Control, and My Other Experiments in Everyday Life"

Gretchen Rubin, "The Happiness Project: Or, Why I Spent a Year Trying to Sing in the Morning, Clean My Closets, Fight Right, Read Aristotle, and Generally Have More Fun"

Sheryl Sandberg, "Lean In: Women, Work, and The Will To Lead"

Brigid Schulte, "Overwhelmed: Work, Love, and Play when No One Has the Time"

Jennifer L. Scott, "Lessons from Madame Chic: 20 Stylish Secrets I Learned While Living in Paris"

Darla Shine, "Happy Housewife: I Was a Whining, Miserable, Desperate Housewife—But I Finally Snapped Out of It. You Can Do It Too."

Jen Sincero, "You Are a Badass: How to Stop Doubting Your Greatness and Start Living an Awesome Life"

Wendy Suzuki, Ph.D., "Healthy Brain, Happy Life: A Personal Program to Activate Your Brain and Do Everything Better"

Mathilde Thomas, "The French Beauty Solution: Time-Tested Secrets to Look and Feel Beautiful Inside and Out"

Brian Tracy, "Change Your Thinking, Change Your Life: How to Unlock Your Full Potential for Success and Achievement"

Brian Tracy, "No Excuses: The Power of Self-Discipline. 21 Ways To Achieve Lasting Happiness and Success"

Sarah Turner, "The Unmumsy Mum: The Hilarious Highs and Emotional Lows of Motherhood"

Laura Vanderkam, "I Know How She Does It: How Successful Women Make the Most of Their Time"

Oprah Winfrey, "The Wisdom of Sundays: Life-Changing Insights From Super Soul Conversations"

Anthony Youn, with Eve Adamson, "The Age Fix: A Leading Plastic Surgeon Reveals How to Really Look 10 Years Younger"

Rachel Zoe with Rose Apodaca, "Style A to Zoe: The Art of Fashion, Beauty, & Everything Glamour"

Bibliography

PART 1

Henry Ramírez-Hoffmann, M.D., "Popular Beliefs About Self-care During the Puerperium, at Level 1 Health Institutions" accessed January 28, 2017 https://www.monografias.com/trabajos905/creencias-populares-puerperio/creencias-populares-puerperio2.shtml

Juliana Rojas H, "Regain your Body after Childbirth with the Indigenous Diet" ABC del Bebe, July 13, 2011, accessed January 28, 2017 http://www.abcdelbebe.com/embarazo/recupere-su-cuerpo-despues-del-parto-con-la-dieta-indigena-11591

Luiza DeSouza, "Eat, Play, Sleep: The Essential Guide to Your Baby's First Three Months" (New York, NY: Atria Books, 2015) P 150 - 151

Stephanie Hua, "Healthy Lactation Cookies" Lick My Spoon, July 20, 2016, accessed October 2016 http://lickmyspoon.com/recipes/cookies/healthy-lactation-cookies/

Cameron Diaz and Sandra Bark, "The Longevity Book: The Science of Aging, the Biology of Strength, and the Privilege of Time" (New York, NY: Harper Wave, 2016) P 97

Amy Wicks, "Jessica Alba Wore a Girdle for Three Months to Get Her Body Back Post-Baby" Glamour, April 25, 2013, accessed February 16, 2016 https://www.glamour.com/story/jessica-alba-wore-a-girdle-for

Brené Brown, "Daring Greatly: How the Courage to Be Vulnerable Transforms the Way We Live, Love, Parent, and Lead"

Rachel Margolis & Mikko Myrskylä Margolis, "Parental Well-being Surrounding First Birth as a Determinant of Further Parity Progression (2015) 52: 1147, accessed February 1, 2017 https://doi.org/10.1007/s13524-015-0413-2

Rob Jordan, "Stanford Researchers Find Mental Health Prescription: Nature" Stanford News, accessed February 16, 2017 https://news.stanford.edu/2015/06/30/hiking-mental-health-063015/

Lauren Smith Brody, "The Fifth Trimester, The Working Mom's Guide to Style, Sanity, & Big Success After Baby" (New York, NY: Doubleday, 2016) P 108, 109

"Depression Among Women," Center for Disease Control and Prevention, accessed January 19, 2017 https://www.cdc.gov/reproductivehealth/depression/index.htm

Albert L. Siu, MD, MSPH; and the US Preventive Services Task Force (USPSTF), "Screening for Depression in Adults US Preventive Services Task Force Recommendation Statement" Jama Network, January 26, 2016, accessed January 19, 2017 https://jamanetwork.com/journals/jama/fullarticle/2484345

Dr. Christina Hibbert, "8 Keys to Mental Health Through Exercise" (New York, NY: W.W. Norton & Company, 2016) P 10, 26

PART 2

Roxy Dillon, BSc, MSc, "Bio-Young: Get Younger at a Cellular and Hormonal Level" (New York, NY: Atria Paperback, 2016) P 162, 167

"Exercise for Stress and Anxiety" Anxiety and Depression Association of America, accessed June 19, 2017
https://adaa.org/living-with-anxiety/managing-anxiety/exercise-stress-and-anxiety

Lana Asprey M.D and Dave Asprey, "The Better Baby Book: How to Have a Healthier, Smarter, Happier Baby" (Hoboken, NJ: John Wiley & Sons, Inc., 2013) P 60

Steven L. Miller, Ph.D. "The Best Time for your Coffee," NeuroscineceDC (blog), October 23, 2013, accessed June 5, 2017 http://neurosciencedc.blogspot.com/2013/10/the-best-time-for-your-coffee/

"100 Healthiest Foods to Satisfy Your Hunger" Time Special Edition, June 2017
P 10, 49

"Exercise: A healthy stress reliever" American Physcological Association, accessed June 19, 2017 http://www.apa.org/news/press/releases/stress/2013/exercise.aspx

Krishna Ramanujan, "Keeping track of weight daily may tip scale in your favor" Cornell Chronicle, June 12, 2015, accessed November 7, 2016 http://news.cornell.edu/stories/2015/06/keeping-track-weight-daily-may-tip-scale-your-favor

Lisa Ryan, "Want to lose weight? Get on the scales every day! Consistent self-monitoring 'helps you shift pounds and keep them off'" March 7, 2016, accessed November 1, 2016 http://www.dailymail.co.uk/health/article-3481166/Want-lose-weight-scales-EVERYDAY-Consistent-self-monitoring-helps-shift-pounds-off.html

Charles Duhigg, "Smarter Faster Better: The Secrets of Productivity in Life and Business" (New York, NY: Random House, 2016) P 265 - 266

Kim Vopni, The Fitness Doula, "Why the 'mum bum' isn't all in the jeans" Published April 9, 2014, Updated May 12, 2018 https://www.theglobeandmail.com/life/health-and-fitness/health-advisor/why-the-mum-bum-isnt-all-in-the-jeans/article17904264/

Nora Tobin, "The Best Foods to Eat Before and After Your Workout" Shape, accessed June 23, 2017 https://www.shape.com/healthy-eating/diet-tips/best-foods-eat-and-after-your-workout

PART 3

Charlotte Cho, "The Little Book of Skin Care: Korean Beauty Secrets for Healthy, Glowing Skin" (New York, NY: William Morrow, 2015) P 100

Mathilde Thomas, "The French Beauty Solution: Time-Tested Secrets to Look and Feel Beautiful Inside and Out" (New York, NY: Avery, 2015) P 149

"Study: Most Americans don't use sunscreen" American Academy of Dermatology, May 19, 2015, accessed September 12, 2016 https://www.aad.org/media/news-releases/study-most-americans-don-t-use-sunscreen

Susan Scutti, "Youthful Skin Comes From Avoiding The Sun; Sleep, Exercise, And Drinking Water Won't Help" Medical Daily, March 4, 2016, accessed, September 21, 2016, https://www.medicaldaily.com/youthful-skin-sun-376560

Harold Lancer M.D., "Younger: The Breakthrough Anti-Aging Method for Radiant Skin" (New York, NY: Grand Central Life & Style 2014) P 36

Roxy Dillon, BSc, MSc, "Bio-Young: Get Younger at a Cellular and Hormonal Level" (New York, NY: Atria Paperback, 2016) P 197

Roxy Dillon, BSc, MSc, "Bio-Young: Get Younger at a Cellular and Hormonal Level" (New York, NY: Atria Paperback, 2016) P 149, 150

Anthony Youn M.D, with Eve Adamson, "The Age Fix: A Leading Plastic Surgeon Reveals How to Really Look 10 Years Younger" (New York, NY: Grand Central Life & Style) P 42

Justin McCarthy and Alyssa Brown, "Getting More Sleep Linked to Higher Well-Being" Gallup, March 2, 2015, accessed August 14, 2017 https://news.gallup.com/poll/181583/getting-sleep-linked-higher.aspx

Arianna Huffington, "The Sleep Revolution: Transforming your Life, One Night at a Time" (New York, NY: Gale, Cengage Learning) P 43, 44, 153 (large print edition)

Chris Stipes, "Artificial Light From Digital Devices Lessens Sleep Quality" University of Houston, July 24, 2017, accessed August 14, 2017 http://www.uh.edu/news-events/stories/2017/july/07242017bluelight.php

"Trends in Consumer Mobility Report" Bank of America, 2015, accessed August 14, 2017 https://promo.bankofamerica.com/mobilityreport/assets/images/2015-Trends-in-Consumer-Mobility-Report_FINAL.pdf

Dun-Xian Tan Rudiger Hardeland Lucien C. Manchester, Ahmet Korkmaz, Shuran Ma, Sergio Rosales-Corral, Russel J. Reiter, "Journal of Experimental Botany, Functional roles of melatonin in plants, and perspectives in nutritional and agricultural science" January 2012, accessed October 23, 2016 https://doi.org/10.1093/jxb/err256

Pamela Druckerman, "Bringing Up Bebé: One American Mother Discovers the Wisdom of French Parenting" (New York, NY: Penguin Books, 2012) P 52, 53

PART 4

Diane Swanbrow, "Ten Minutes of Talking has a Mental Payoff" Michigan News, University of Michigan, October 29, 2007, accessed April 12, 2017 https://news.umich.edu/ten-minutes-of-talking-has-a-mental-payoff

Jessica Joelle Alexander & Iben Dissing Sandahl, "The Danish Way of Parenting: What Happiest People in the World Know About Raising Confident, Capable Kids" (New York NY: TarcherPerigee, 2016) P 133

David Spiegel, "Breast Cancer, Mind Body Connection, Importance of Support Groups" May 27, 2013, accessed October 22, 2017 https://www.youtube.com/watch?v=uOJ6OTieANQ

Bonnie Milletto, "Girlfriends are Good for your Health: Stanford University, Mind-Body Connection - The Benefits of Female Relationships" July 30, 2017, accessed October 22, 2017 https://www.thriveglobal.com/stories/10369-girlfriends-are-good-for-your-health

Brian Tracy, "No Excuses: The Power of Self-Discipline. 21 Ways To Achieve Lasting Happiness and Success" (New York, NY: MJF Books, 2010) P 189

Chris Bailey, "The Productivity Project: Accomplishing More by Managing your Time, Attention, and Energy" Crown Publishing Group, (New York, NY: Crown Publishing Group, 2016) P 36, 37, 76

Brigid Schulte, "Overwhelmed: Work, Love, and Play When No One Has The Time" (New York, NY: Sarah Crichton Books, 2014) P 249

Sheryl Sandberg, "Lean In: Women, Work, and The Will To Lead" (New York, NY: Alfred A. Knopf, 2013) P 94, 113

John M. Gottman, Ph.D., and Julie Schwartz Gottman, Ph.D., "And Baby Makes Three. The Six-Step Plan for Preserving Marital Intimacy and Rekindling Romance After Baby Arrives" (New York, NY: Crown Publishers, 2017) P 9

"Should Parents Post Photos of Their Children on Social Media?" The Wall Street Journal, May 23, 2016 https://www.wsj.com/articles/should-parents-post-photos-of-their-children-on-social-media-1463968922

Chris Weller, "A former Google Executive Reveals Tricks Tech Companies Use to Grab Attention" Business Insider, August 28, 2017 http://www.businessinsider.com/why-phones-are-addicting-according-to-former-google-exec-2017-8

Marie Kondo, "The Life-Changing Magic of Tidying Up" (Farmington Hills, MI: Gale Cengage Learning) 60-62 (large print edition)

Sue McGreevey, "Eight weeks to a better brain" The Harvard Gazette, January 21, 2011 https://news.harvard.edu/gazette/story/2011/01/eight-weeks-to-a-better-brain/

Bhante Gunaratana, "Mindfulness in Plain English" (Somerville, MA: Wisdom Publications, 2011) P 146

Richard Louv, "Vitamin N: The Essential Guide To a Nature-Rich Life" (New York: NY: Algonquin Books of Chapel Hill, 2015) P 155, 156

Shonda Rhimes, "My year of Saying Yes to Everything" TED 2016 https://www.ted.com/talks/shonda_rhimes_my_year_of_saying_yes_to_everything/discussion?rss&utm_

James Hakner, "Misery of work second only to illness" University of Sussex, February 2, 2016, accessed November 1, 2016, (A 2016 joint study by the University of Sussex and the London School of Economics) http://www.sussex.ac.uk/broadcast/read/34072

Meg Meeker, M.D., "The 10 Habits of Happy Mothers: Reclaiming Our Passion, Purpose, and Sanity" (New York, NY: Ballantine Books, 2010) P 113

Brian Tracy, "Change Your Thinking, Change Your Life: How to Unlock Your Full Potential for Success and Achievement" (New York, NY: MJF Books, 2010) P10

Gretchen Rubin, "The Happiness Project: Or, Why I Spent a Year Trying to Sing in the Morning, Clean My Closets, Fight Right, Read Aristotle, and Generally Have More Fun" (New York, NY: Harper, 2009) P 223

About the Author

Sara Gaviria is a Colombian journalist with an MA in Marketing and Communications from Westminster University, U.K. She lived in London in her twenties and in California in her thirties. She worked as an advertising executive for media publications in London and for *The San Diego Union-Tribune* for six years, serving in her last position as a Manager of Hispanic Publications. She currently lives in Houston, Texas, with her husband and son.